ODEON

RELICS

ODEON Relics: Nineteen-Thirties Icons in the Twenty-First Century

Published in Great Britain in 2019 by Art Deco Magpie.

Designed by Philip Butler.

Edited & proofread by Joanne Halliday.

Printed by Swallowtail Print, Norfolk, U.K.

A CIP Catalogue record for this book is available from the British Library.

The publisher gratefully acknowledges the financial support of the online community who have pledged via Kickstarter.com to help make this book become a reality. Please see the supporters list on page 144.

ISBN: 978-1-9997596-1-2

This book and its authors are in no way affiliated with the Odeon Cinemas Group - a subsidiary of AMC Theatres. It has been produced independently with no involvement or endorsement from either organisation.

ART DECO MAGPIE
artdecomagpie.com

FSC
www.fsc.org
MIX
Paper from responsible sources
FSC® C113523

ODEON
RELICS

FUNNY GIRLS
wilko

FOREWORD

NEON NORTHERN LIGHTS

'Blackpool: Home of The Famous Illuminations.' It's not a destination I'd given much thought to before last year. Don't get me wrong, I'm not adverse to basking in the rain at one of Britain's many fading coastal 'resorts.' However, Blackpool, with its reputation for raucous hen nights, miles of multicolour bulbs, and acres of gambling arcades, had never really appealed. Despite my scepticism, last October I found myself Blackpool-bound like millions of holidaymakers before me – family in tow – to see for myself what this notorious destination had to offer. Apart from introducing my young daughters to the addictive joys of the penny pushers, my primary motivation was an ongoing project to retrace the footsteps of legendary architectural photographer John Maltby.

In 1935, having recently moved down from Birkenhead, 25 year old Maltby set up a photographic studio in a London basement. That same year he gained a commission that would put him on the map; to document the rapidly expanding Odeon cinema estate. Maltby's eye for composition and his technical ability, combined with the startling subject matter, helped kick-start his career. He Became one of the most important English architectural photographers of the twentieth century. Now held in The National Archives, his atmospheric monochrome portfolio gives a priceless window into how the pioneering architecture of the period looked when new, free from alteration and before years of neglect and decay. Inspired by Maltby's work, I set myself the task of documenting the 1930s Odeon estate in the twenty-first century, or at least, what was left of it.

Truth be told, Maltby himself never actually shot the 1939 Blackpool Odeon, having fallen out with founder Oscar Deutsch some months earlier over a billing discrepancy. Nevertheless, to complete my project, Blackpool was, for better or worse, unavoidable.

380ft up, from the top of Blackpool's world-famous tower, I caught my first glimpse of the old cinema. Despite changes in the urban landscape over the intervening years, its mass still dominates the surrounding area. Returning to examine it closer after dark, the voluminous elegance really hit home. A sheer face of cream faience tiles rose up from a huge canopy studded with blinking bulbs. Pink neon signs buzzed aloft in the darkness advertising the current business Funny Girls, a cabaret club that opened after the building ceased screening films in the late 1990s. Crossing the road to take my shot, I admired the evolution from 1930s hi-tech picture house to kitsch seaside attraction; arguably the perfect reinvention of the space considering its location.

The cinema industry has moved on over the last 80 years and many of these old picture palaces have been demolished. Of the 140 built and opened under the Odeon banner before the outbreak of war in 1939, only 52 survive in their entirety, with a handful of others remaining in altered form. This book celebrates those survivors in an attempt to both capture their particular beauty, and to investigate their individual journeys. Regardless of how you feel about the fate of these 'relics', I hope you can still appreciate their majesty and marvel at the bold vision Oscar Deutsch and his talented associates shared all those years ago.

Philip Butler - June 2019

ODEON
TO DAY
DICK
POWELL
HAPPINESS
AHEAD
FOR
ODEON
ODEON
THEATRE
ENTIRELY BRITISH
WE OFFER YOU FILMS OF SUCH
STAGGERING ENTERTAINMENT VALUE
AS ALMOST TO BEGGAR DESCRIPTION
ONLY THE ODEON

JUST 'ROUND THE CORNER AT THE ODEON

How Oscar Deutsch commissioned Great Britain's most progressive picture palaces

By Jason Sayer

No other cinema chain has enjoyed such cultural success and longevity as Odeon. Its presence spans generations and geographies across Great Britain with its bold architecture — ubiquitous iconicity — often being as entertaining as the moving pictures shown inside. In its inter-war heyday it was an experience to enter an Odeon, a place to which one could escape from the drudgeries of everyday life, economic worries and fear over escalating international tensions. They were considered community assets, running popular Saturday morning shows for children. Restaurants' usually housed on the upper foyers, added to allure, making the cinema somewhere you could while away the hours with friends. Before each screening an announcer would come onto the stage and introduce the programme, and at the end the National Anthem would play. The Odeon chain even had its own song which was routinely performed by the organist who serenaded audiences before films were shown.

Won't you meet me tonight /
Where your favourite, past-time's right /
It's 'round the corner at the O-de-on /
Just 'round the corner at the O-de-on

Over a mere 11 years, founder Oscar Deutsch opened a staggering 258 Odeons, of which 140 were new builds. At the zenith of its popularity in 1940, 100 million patrons passed through Odeon's doors. To put that figure into perspective, only 54 million cinema tickets were sold in total in the UK in 1984. Although attendance figures have since improved, the slump compared to the heyday of 1.64 billion ticket sales in 1946[1] had a significant impact on the British cinema industry. Many chains had to radically downsize to remain in business and Odeon was no exception.

This book is not a definitive history of the Odeon chain, its cinemas or its founder. Rather, it provides context for the iconic structures built by the chain at its apex that still survive today, which have been beautifully documented by photographer Philip Butler.

Left: **ISLEWORTH** (1935)
by George Coles

On Monday 1 October 1928, the Picture House at Brierley Hill in Staffordshire opened with two silent movies: the Anglo-German comedy crime co-production, *The Ghost Train*, and the American movie *Woman on Trial*. Even before opening, it caused a stir in the community. Designed in an Assyrian style by local architect Stanley Griffiths, the theatre was set back from the high street and was "the grandest in the area."[2] Down the road, older rival auditorium, the Palace, put on the ever-popular *Ben Hur* to divert attention from the Picture House's opening furore.

The most defining aspect of the Picture House at Brierley Hill, wasn't apparent at the time of its opening however. It was the first cinema to be built by Oscar Deutsch, the son of Hungarian immigrant and Jewish scrap metal merchant Leopold Deutsch.

Though a fashionably modern industry for the time, cinema was nothing new to Oscar Deutsch. He once lived above a man called Sol Levy, a businessman and film magnate who had built theatres in Birmingham and Liverpool, both trading as the Scala. Levy also ran the Futurist, opening in 1919 it became the first cinema in Birmingham to put on 'talkies' in 1929. The pair were part of the same Jewish community and it's likely Sol was an influence on the young Deutsch who soon followed suit, taking over a pair of old movie theatres in Coventry before entering the new build market.

Though considered opulent for the area, the Brierley Hill Picture House was decidedly modest compared to what he had in store for the rest of the West Midlands and, indeed, the country.

It was another two years before Deutsch opened his next cinema at Perry Barr, north Birmingham: a building designed in a Moorish style by Griffiths, this time working with Horace G. Bradley. It was this distinctive cinema, with the benefit of hindsight, that was the biggest indication of what was to come. Deutsch had planned to use the Picture House name again. However, the owners of the nearby Birchfield Picture House objected. Deutsch needed a new name.

Cue Mel Mindelsohn, who had assisted with setting up the Brierley Hill cinema. He had spotted a name whilst on holiday in Tunis: 'Odeon.' It was exotic — Ancient Greek for 'singing place' — yet not totally alienating to English speakers. Coincidentally, it started with Oscar Deutch's initials, leading later to the advertising backronym 'Oscar Deutsch Entertains Our Nation.'

Two cinemas in two years, though, wasn't exactly breathtaking considering the rapid rate at which rivals were building across the country. The Moorish quality of Perry Barr was also stylistically old fashioned compared to pioneering examples of the period like the New Victoria Cinema in London (now known as the Apollo) which had opened in the same year. For that, architects William Edward Trent and E. Wamsley Lewis had drawn upon the modern cinemas and theatres in Europe, and in particular, Germany; The Großes Schauspielhaus in Berlin (1919) by Hans Poelzig as well as his Deli-Kino in Wrocław (1927); The Titania-Palast (1927) also in Berlin by Schöffler, Schloenbach und Jacobi; and the Universum or 'Schaubühne' by Erich Mendelsohn (1928) in Berlin too. Such work, along with similar projects carried out by the aforementioned architects, was regularly appearing in the architectural press and receiving praise.

Modernist auditoriums were just the tip of the iceberg in Germany, where the Deutscher Werkbund (German Association of Craftsmen) was keen to foster a sense of progression. In 1911, architect Walter Gropius joined Adolf Meyer to work on the Fagus Factory in Alfeld. The sleek factory with glass walls adhered to Gropius' idea of architecture having a dominant social function – "palaces of labour" with "light, fresh air with hygienic condition."[3] Gropius went on to found the infamous Bauhaus school in 1919 and, alongside contemporaries such as Swiss-French architect Le Corbusier and Austrian-Czech architect Adolf Loos, became a pioneer of a style known as Modernism which championed new materials, rational form, and the removal of ornament.

Above: **PERRY BARR** (1930) as it originally looked before major 1950s alterations.

Left: **OSCAR DEUTSCH** : A workaholic in the his office; captured on 7th May 1938 for Associated Newspapers.

In The Netherlands, the Amsterdam School style of Expressionist architecture was also garnering international acclaim. Characterized by brick construction with complicated masonry and rounded streamline forms, it became favoured in the design of schools, housing estates, municipal institutions and department stores from as early as 1910.

Meanwhile in Paris, the 1925 Exposition Internationale des Art Décoratifs et Industriels Modernes — from which we get the term Art Deco — showcased a great menagerie of progressive design and decoration. Furniture, interiors, architecture and works of art all borrowed forms and motifs from Egyptian and Assyrian archaeology; Howard Carter had discovered the tomb of Tutankhamun only three years earlier, spearheading a commercial boom resonating throughout the design world.

But off the continent in Britain, certainly within the architectural sphere, Modernism and Art Deco were slow to arrive. Britain was still transfixed by the Arts and Crafts movement and neo-traditional design. In 1925, architect Peter Behrens designed a one-off Modernist white – the colour of purists – house: 'New Ways' in Northampton. It didn't make an impact, the *Architectural Review* describing it only as an "exercise in modernity."[4] Scorn came from both sides as well, with Modernists dismissing Art Deco as merely fashion, a phenomenon wholly withdrawn from function.

It took Frank Pick, CEO of the London Passenger Transport Board (LPTB, the predecessor of Transport for London) to commission architects with an eye for modernity. Pick was inspired by a trip to Germany and Scandinavia in 1930 with the architect Charles Holden where the pair witnessed the architectural avant-garde in action. Holden had designed many stations on the Northern line, starting with Clapham Common in 1924, but while modern, these were reserved in style. He would go on to design many ground-breaking tube stations for Pick, with Sudbury Town, the first after their European tour, being more in-step with continental Modernism.

Above: **WORTHING** (1934) by Whinny, Son & Austin Hall
Demolished in 1986.

Left: **SOUTH HARROW** (1933) by A. P. Starkey.
Majority demolished in 1972, although the two retail wings on either side remain.

Though Deutsch would later gain a reputation for constructing equally progressive buildings, his next few cinemas didn't allude to this at the time. The Royal in Alfreton (1931) was a neo-traditional offering — the façade being mock Tudor — but inside, architect Harry Clayton had designed a fashionable Art Deco auditorium. Clayton worked on the next Odeon cinema too, a conversion of a bus garage in Weymouth (1933). Again it was nothing special, nowhere near as grand in scale as Perry Barr or as forward thinking as what was going up in Germany.

Perhaps it was the Art Deco cinema being built in Kingston, Southwest London, designed by James E. Adamson (of the Marshall & Tweedy practice) that wet Deutsch's appetite for stylistic experimentation. The theatre, mixing Moorish and Modernist features on its façade, was set to be independently operated, but Deutsch saw a business opportunity and purchased the building during construction. This meant that only a month after an Odeon in Weymouth had opened, so too had the Odeon Kingston. Deutsch was to repeat this trick several times going forward, snapping up sites with pre-approved planning permission or partly built shells to accelerate expansion.

Now Deutsch was beginning to set his pace. 1933 saw five Odeon cinemas open. It was the fourth that ushered in the Odeon 'house style;' the Streamline Moderne aesthetic now synonymous with Odeon. Arthur Percival Starkey — known as A. P. Starkey — was the architect and designed his first cinema for Deutsch in his hometown of South Harrow. Starkey used faience tiles which could be easily cleaned for the sleek, low-rise building, while the streamlined aesthetic amplified its length. The entrance was recessed and with two wings either side housing shops and a café.

The cinema was a success and set Deutsch in his stride. 16 Odeons were to open the following year, with Starkey and his associate Frederick Adkins working on six of the new cinemas in outer London suburbs between 1934 and 1935. The cinemas were indicative of the stylistic swing in Europe, particularly in London where new underground stations like those at Boston Manor, Southgate and Arnos Grove, designed by Charles Holden, adopted a similar streamlined Expressionist look.

Economy was also a key factor in Odeon construction. "Every effort was made to build the Odeons at Colindale, Sudbury Town, Wealdstone, North Finchley, Sidcup and Reading at a very economical figure,"[5] remarked Adkins on the Odeon empire's expansion. Inside, stadium style seating was used for the auditoriums, negating the need for an expensive girder supporting a balcony. As a result, Deutsch's early cinemas cost around £20,000 — less than half the typical cost of a cinema at the time.[6]

WARLEY
TODAY WE LIVE AGAIN HIS GREATEST GAMBLE A

The model from the Odeon South Harrow was borrowed for most of these, as the symmetrical wings with cafés and shops were able to supply additional revenue streams for the cinema.

Along with building cheaper cinemas, Deutsch sold ground rents, most notably to the Prudential and Eagle Star[7] insurance companies, to raise capital to help finance the rapid expansion[8]. He brokered 19 deals with Eagle Star between 1935 and 1938. Under these deals, each Odeon was run as an individual company, meaning that if one failed it didn't bring the whole empire down with it. This model also saw a large minority of shares being owned by local business people including the proprietors of shops and cafés within the premises.

However, while Starkey and Adkins provided the architectural framework for Odeon's initial progress, it was architect Harry Weedon with who he had the most fruitful relationship.

Deutsch met Weedon while the architect was working on a new building for Deutsch's late father's metalwork firm Deutsch & Brenner in Hockley. Weedon had also grown up in Birmingham, even going to the same grammar school as Deutsch. Despite being a local, he had essentially been exiled from the area after having an affair with a neighbour's wife. The couple later moved to Leamington where Weedon worked briefly as a manager at a catering firm. He went to Birmingham on business and, as chance would have it, bumped into a member of his former Masonic lodge whose friendly greeting signified he was welcome back in his hometown.

Having hit it off, Weedon enthusiastically accepted an invitation from Deutsch to work on the interiors[9] for the Odeon at Warley, Staffordshire in 1934. It was to be the start of a prolific partnership.

13 new build Odeon cinemas opened in 1935, three less than the year before. But, in 1936, a staggering 35 were unveiled and this feat was repeated the following year. Such relentless growth epitomised Deutsch: a workaholic, he was frustrated when progress was slow. This possibly explains the seemingly sporadic purchase of old cinemas — a far cry from the sleek modern image he was curating — from 1935 onwards to maintain growth.

Before leaving Birmingham, Weedon had practiced as a commercial architect. He designed factories and was experienced with quick turnarounds. To meet Deutsch's demands, Weedon delegated most of the design work to his staff. He worked closely with his chief assistants, John Cecil Clavering and later Robert Bullivant, who were part of a 140-

Left: **WARLEY** (1934) by
Thomas Cecil Howitt.
Demolished 1970.

Below: **BURNLEY** (1937) by
Robert Bullivant.
Demolished 2005.

-strong office. Prior to meeting Deutsch, Weedon only employed six staff. As his firm grew, he employed young graduates fresh from university. Clavering, by example, was only 23 when he joined. To ensure efficiency, Weedon provided his staff with bespoke boxwood drawing scales that highlighted measurements for cinema seating.

The homegrown Odeon style, meanwhile, created by Starkey, Clavering, and Bullivant, as well as architects George Coles, P. J. Price, W. Calder Robson, Andrew Mather, Thomas Braddock and Thomas Cecil Howitt. Faience tiling was the favoured façade material, as it remained unblemished by the smoke and smog of the industrial towns Deutsch built in, and could be employed in tandem with rounded corners for a streamline finish. When this couldn't be done, usually due to council objections, brick was used in an Expressionist fashion, as can be see with the extant examples in York and Chester. A vertical feature, sometimes an advertising tower, was another trademark Odeon element. Neon was used to highlight the linearity of the design at night so as to ensure aesthetic continuity.

Work progressed at a staggering pace, with multiple schemes developed concurrently. Speaking to Allen Eyles of *Focus on Film* in 1975, Bullivant recalled a 9 p.m. phone call when Weedon asked him to visit a site in Falmouth. He drove 400 miles through the night for an impromptu meeting the following morning. Within three weeks, plans for the scheme had been approved and Odeon Falmouth was completed less than a year later.

While the modern architecture of the LPTB was confined to the nodes of the transport network stretching from London into Buckinghamshire and Hertfordshire — an area dubbed 'Metro-land' — Deutsch's cinemas reached much further. In many towns, cinemas were the only piece of forward-thinking architecture they had. As in Falmouth — a traditional Cornish harbour town — Odeons were often totally at odds with their surroundings, their futuristic forms incongruent but seemingly welcomed by the locals.

Deutsch wasn't afraid of taking risks either. In Corby, he built a cinema in 1936 to attract workers to a newly developing iron-ore field. The Odeon at Dudley (1937), a few miles west of Birmingham, was built along with new council housing, sports grounds and projects such as Dudley Zoo (also completed in 1937 and designed by the infamous architect Berthold Lubetkin's Tecton Group). All were built to a modern design and epitomized the municipal bravery of the time.

To attract customers, Deutsch felt Odeons had to be grander than their counterparts. Souvenir programmes lauded their design, going into some detail about their architecture and the architect behind them. The flagship Leicester Square Odeon (1937) proudly featured Weedon's design as a silhouette on the cover. Inside, Deutsch wrote:

"It is with a sense of great pride and gratitude that I welcome you to this new theatre... pride in the fact that this theatre belongs to the Odeon circuit and in the knowledge that British goods and workmen have erected such a magnificent building ...gratitude to the men that designed this theatre and to those that have carried out these designs so successfully."[10]

Although built on a tight budget, Deutsch was eager to not compromise aesthetics. He refused to allow film posters to dominate the façades of his cinemas; the advertising being explicitly secondary to the architectural language. Deutsch was aware of the impact his cinemas were making too. Speaking in *Architectural Design and Construction*, he said:

"It was always my ambition to have buildings which were individual and striking, but which were always objects of architectural beauty. ...We endeavour to make our buildings express the fact that they are specially erected as the homes of the latest, most progressive entertainment in the world today ... I am determined and every member of my organisation from the highest to the lowest is fully aware of the fact, that every future theatre we build will be better ...than its predecessor."[11]

Above: **LEICESTER SQUARE** (1937)
auditorium before later alterations.

Top Left: **FALMOUTH** (1936)
by P. J. Price.
Demolished 1976.

Left: **CHINGFORD** (1935) by Andrew Mather. Demolished in 1972.

So proud was Deutsch of his growing estate, that he kept a visual record by employing photographer John Maltby, who was paid five guineas to shoot the exteriors and interiors of each Odeon.

Inside, Odeons often featured innovative atmospheric lighting arrangements; illuminated ceiling coves, linear lanterns, and coloured floodlights paired with reflective surfaces served to enchant the audience. They were turned on gradually after screenings until the whole theatre was flooded with light.

Deutsch called his staff Lieutenants and gave them uniforms that matched the décor of the cinema — unusual at the time when staff were typically expected to wear their own clothing. At Perry Barr, ankle jewellery, veils and turbans were worn to complement the Moorish architecture. Such exotic attention to detail was often a hit in the English suburban towns.

Deutsch was aware he was cultivating an audience as attracted by the comfort of his buildings as the films he put on. His wife Lily, described as having an "excellent eye for colour and design... Especially gold!"[12] was involved with colour palettes and fabric choices, helping to create an air of luxury achieved at a modest cost.

Small affordable indulgences such as an evening in a warm comfortable cinema during this largely austere period between two World Wars cannot be understated; there were reports of families attending the same film, several nights in a row simply to escape the cold inhospitable conditions at home.[13]

Despite once selling 100 million tickets in a year, Odeon's popularity wasn't to last. Following Oscar's untimely death from cancer in 1941, ownership passed to the Rank Organisation. With a cinema-heavy portfolio that also contained over 300 theatres from the once rival Gaumont chain, paired with falling attendances, Rank started to close and sell off Odeons as early as the 1950s.

31 years after opening, Deutsch's first cinema at Brierley Hill was demolished and replaced by a supermarket. The building in Perry Barr remains, albeit not as a cinema. Before being converted into the Royale Banqueting Suite, it was turned into a bingo hall in 1968, a fate many others, such as the impressive Grade II listed Odeon Kingstanding (1935) shared.

Kingstanding joins 20 other listed former Odeons, including a Grade II* example at Muswell Hill in London. Ten of these cinemas are no longer used for their primary function, being either vacant, a church, or consigned to being a bingo hall.

"It's getting increasingly difficult to add listings," says Elain Harwood, C20th architectural historian with Historic England. "[Authorities] feel as if they covered the subject 20 years ago and that enough are already listed."[14]

Unlisted Odeons have been subject to much more extensive alterations, as can be see with the former cinema at Balham, London. The auditorium was demolished in 1985 and the building was repurposed as a Majestic Wine Warehouse; its impressive faience frontage, a massive giveaway to its past life, remains.

The former Odeon at Isleworth has also kept its façade but has been transformed, becoming the entrance to flats built on the auditorium site, which does little to pay respects to the old cinema. Similarly, at Hanley and Bristol, the shells have been retained, but the interiors gutted to house a nightclub and retail units.

Other Odeons haven't been quite so fortunate. Once impressive cinemas at Ramsgate, Burnley, St Austell and, particularly, Erith, Bury St Edmunds, Chingford, Surbiton and Colwyn Bay have all been lost. Even gaining coveted listed status wasn't enough to save the fine example at Worthing, where developers successfully overturned the protection prior to flattening it. Most of this demolition work was carried out in the 1970s and 1980s as the cinema industry declined, though those at Aylesbury and Hackney Road suffered the wrecking ball as recently as 2017 and 2018 respectively. A big blow for Deutsch — had he still been alive — would have been the demolition of his prized local Odeon at Warley, torn down in 1970.

Such losses demonstrate the difficulties of repurposing a building like a cinema. Deutsch's cinemas, as well as others, eschewed building in adaptability to save money and so couldn't be easily be altered to accommodate stage productions, thus limiting their future viability significantly.

The popularity of high-street bingo is also waning as online gambling becomes increasingly favoured[15]. It's not all bad news, however. While bingo may be on the way out, cinema appears to be making a comeback. 2018 saw 177 million patrons purchase cinema tickets in the UK — the highest attendance rate since the 1970s. Boutique cinema chains such as Everyman and Picturehouse are breathing new life into older cinemas and bringing back the glamour of a night at the pictures. It may not be time to start building again, but it certainly seems time to appreciate the surviving picture palaces already gifted to us.

Above: **BRISTOL** by Thomas Cecil Howitt. A composite photograph (1938 / 2017)

ODEON RELICS

A PHOTOGRAPHIC SERIES OF THE SURVIVORS

November 2017 - July 2019

SURVIVING CINEMAS BUILT BY OSCAR DEUTSCH/ODEON
(1928-1956) listed chronologically by opening date

2 Perry Barr
8 Lancing
15 Wallington
18 Bognor Regis
22 Welling
25 Colindale
27 Isleworth
30 Barnet
31 Weston-Super-Mare
32 Kingstanding
40 Faversham
41 Corby
42 Scarborough
43 Sutton Coldfield
46 Well Hall
51 Bridgwater
52 Deal
53 Southall
56 Ashford
57 Ipswich
58 Muswell Hill
61 Bromley
62 Harrogate
63 Chester
64 Stafford
70 Loughborough
71 Portsmouth
73 Sittingbourne
76 York
77 Hanley
78 Forest Gate
80 Wrexham
83 Yeovil
89 Dudley
91 Bournemouth
96 Exeter
97 Peterborough
98 Morecambe
99 Swiss Cottage
100 Wolverhampton
101 Woolwich
102 Rhyl
103 Leicester Square
109 Chorley
112 Newport
114 Eltham Hill
115 Balham
118 Llanelli
120 Halifax
122 Bristol
123 East Ham
125 Leicester
126 Ayr
128 Luton
137 Blackpool
141 Worcester
142 Saint Helier
145 Sheffield

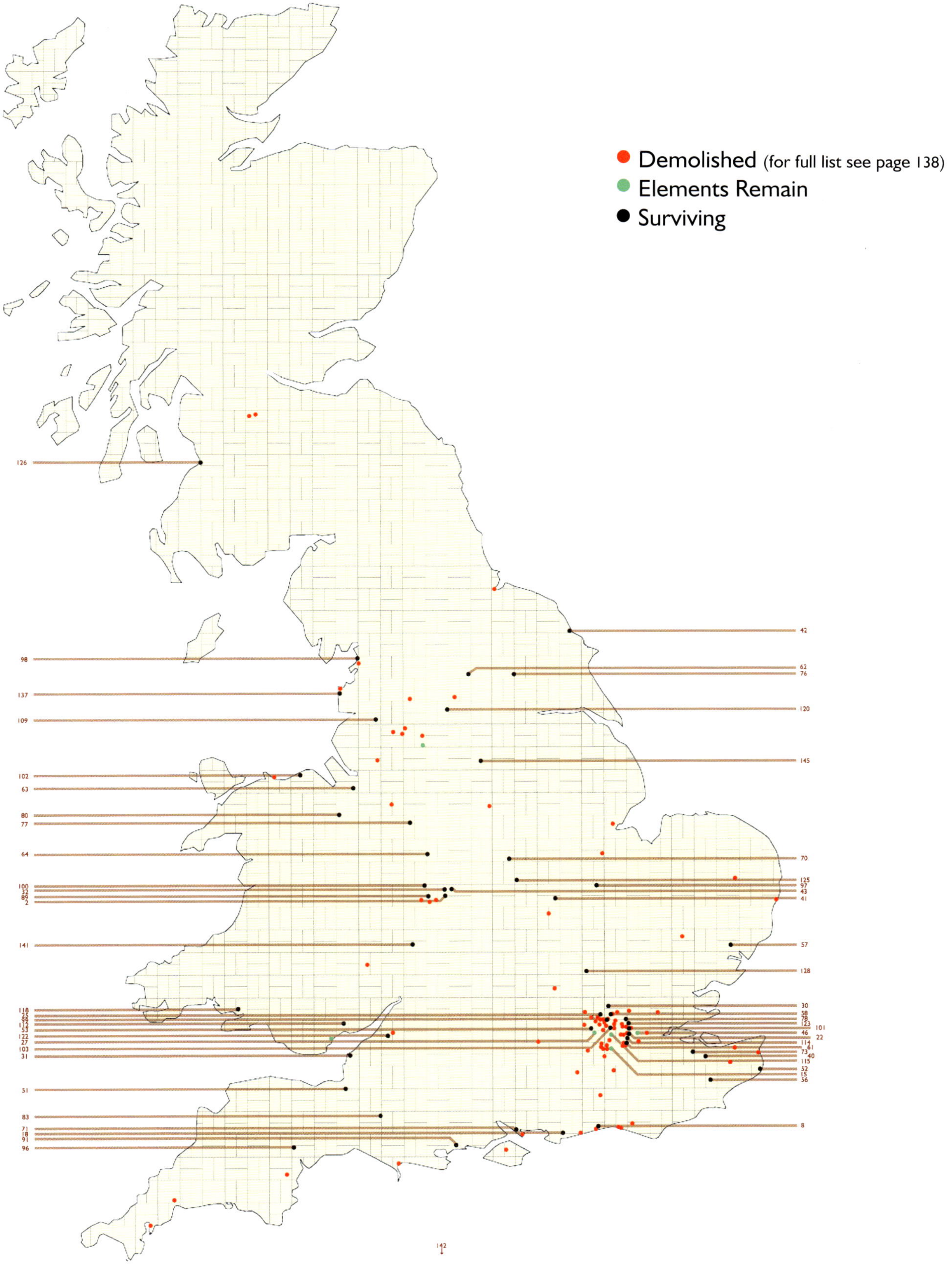

Demolished (for full list see page 138)
Elements Remain
Surviving
126
98
137
109
102
63
80
77
64
100
32
89
2
141
118
25
53
122
27
103
31
51
83
71
18
91
96
42
62
76
120
145
70
125
97
43
41
57
128
30
58
78
123
101
46
22
114
61
73
40
115
52
15
56
8
142

O2 PERRY BARR

271 Birchfield Road, Birmingham, B20 3DD
1930 / Stanley A. Griffiths & Horace G. Bradley

The concept for the first Odeon was an exotic theme cinema with patrons encouraged to fully immerse themselves in the escapism that the silver screen offered. The front of the building was designed to resemble a Western take on a North African mosque (see page 9), and the auditorium was decorated with Moorish murals and sumptuous drapes. To compound the experience, ushers and usherettes were required to wear Moroccan style garments finished with anklets, veils, and turbans.

The Perry Barr area, like much of Birmingham, suffered heavy bombing during the war. In an attempt to disguise this easily distinguishable white landmark, the façade was painted in camouflage hues for the duration. Despite this precaution, the building didn't escape the conflict unscathed. Rather than restore the original frontage, it was replaced with the sharp mid-century brick façade in 1953 that can still be seen today.

The cinema continued to be run as an Odeon by the Rank Organisation until 1969 when it transferred the property to its Top Rank Bingo arm. Closed in 1983, it changed hands several times over the following years but continued to be primarily used for bingo until the turn of the Millennium. After sitting vacant for five years, it reopened in 2002 as the Royale Banqueting Suite.

ROYALE SUITE
ROYALE SUITE
0121 356 9944

O8 LANCING

45 Penhill Road, Lancing, BN15 8HA
1933 / unknown architect

1933 saw the launch of the 'Odeon circuit,' a rapidly growing series of cinemas run as separate companies showing much the same roster of films. The planning of these early cinemas had been underway for well over twelve months but, in what would become a regular occurrence, Deutsch bought out a cinema already under construction in Lancing. With design and planning already compete, this may have seemed a shrewd method of hastily increasing the number of brand new Odeons opening, but the logic in this particular venture was flawed given that a much larger, more contemporary Odeon was already under construction just three miles away in Worthing!

Designed by a local unrecorded architect arranged by the builders A.W. Gates & Son Ltd, the Lancing Odeon had an unassuming and traditional appearance. It housed two shops and a café above the foyer, and could seat 691 people (the smallest Odeon constructed). It seems that Deutsch quickly became embarrassed by the cinema as his family of Modernist masterpieces continued to expand across the country; by 1936 it had been renamed the Regal in attempt to distance itself from both the brand and its more illustrious Worthing sibling. In 1939, the cinema was leased out for six years to independent operators, but eventually came back under control of the Rank Organisation in 1945. Following a rocky period of stiff competition with the town's Luxor cinema, both were bought out by a London firm who immediately closed the Regal.

Since the 1950s, the building has been home to many different businesses including a chrome-plater, a car showroom, a tanning salon, and a plumbers' merchants to name but a few.

Entrance
ON THE BLUE WALL
impact
3rd Place
Worthing
Gym of the
Year 2017
FUEL

O15 WALLINGTON

25 Ross Parade, Wallington, SM6 8QF
1934 / Yates, Cook & Darbyshire

Yates, Cook, and Darbyshire was a prolific London based multi-disciplinary practice, with architects, engineers & quantity surveyors all in-house, active predominantly during the inter-war and early post-war years. In addition to designing a wide range of other buildings, they were responsible for four Odeons. Arguably none were architecturally exceptional though. Tolworth, Worcester Park & Wimbledon have all long since been demolished, but elements of the Wallington cinema still survive.

Opening in May 1934, the Wallington Odeon had a low Portland stone clad frontage with a curved corner entrance framed by two parallel bands of neon. The auditorium was single storey with a stadium style layout designed to accommodate 935 patrons. The cinema was closed in 1957, and the auditorium was demolished shortly after. A new structure incorporating the original foyer replaced it, opening as a Wallis supermarket. J. D. Wetherspoon have operated a pub named The Whispering Moon from the premises since the late 1990s.

The Whispering Moon
Orchid Nails
CELEBRATIONS FOREVER
Party & Gift Shop
GENTS STYLISTS
GENTS BARBERS
THE WHISPERING MOON
FOOD
FAMILY DINING
WINES
GLOBAL BEERS
ROSS PARADE

O18 BOGNOR REGIS

64 London Road, Bognor Regis, PO21 1PT
1934 / Whinny, Son & Austin Hall

Bognor Regis was home to the second of four Odeons designed by Whinny, Son & Austin Hall. It opened four months after their ground-breaking example in nearby Worthing. Alas, the design here was nowhere near as innovative or striking, but it was not without charm. Like several others that followed, the frontage featured a run of shops with owner accommodation either side of the imposing cinema entrance. Originally this was considerably taller than rest of the façade, clad in buff faience, with four narrow columns rising to a plinth underlining the Odeon sign.

Following disposal by the Rank Organisation in 1971, it was briefly run independently as the Regal cinema before being converted for use a bingo hall. Crown Bingo have operated from the building since 1987. At some point prior to Crown taking over, the faience tiles were removed from the entrance façade and the overall height was reduced. Recently, the neighbouring retail and residential units have been refurbished with the addition of extra front facing windows on the upper storey.

AFFORDABLE
SCAFFOLDING
PETER ARNETT LEISURE
Proudly presents the
BEST IN BINGO
ENTERTAINMENT
Welcome to
CROWN BINGO
CROWN BINGO

O22 WELLING

Upper Wickham Lane, Welling, DA16 3HF
1934 / George Coles

Dalston-born architect George Coles was one of the most respected and well-known cinema designers of the period. Between 1912 and 1939, he was involved with the design of over 90 different venues. A wide range of styles emanated from his practice, and he earned a reputation for being able to work with tight budgets and even tighter deadlines.
Welling was the first of 19 designs that Coles prepared for Odeon, although several other independent cinemas by Coles were later taken over by the chain.

Clad in Portland stone, which has been long since painted over, the façade featured decorative details that had more in common with 1920s Art Deco than the Modernist image Odeon was cultivating at the time. Above the entrance are three recessed leaded glass windows with a recurring 'O' motif. Once stained glass, they are now in a poor state of repair, painted grey, with cracks and broken panes showing a wooden ply backing behind.

Having had a fairly short run as cinema, it closed in 1960 and was transferred to the Top Rank Bingo arm of the Rank Organisation, later becoming a Mecca Bingo. Closing again in 2007, it was resurrected two years later as a church by Freedom Centre International.

FCI
Freedom Centre International
hapel.or
Ofosuware
38
www.tilemates.c
0 7277 8700
Ceramic
Porcelain

O25 COLINDALE

287 Edgeware Road, London, NW9 6NB
1934 / A. P. Starkey

Arthur Percival Starkey was the visionary architect responsible for one of the most important early Odeon designs; South Harrow. It was so successful that the concept was modified for designs in Kingsbury, Sidcup, North Finchley and Colindale. Given that Colindale is the only example left standing in its entirety, it's a shame that it is not preserved in better condition.

Having been closed by the Rank Organisation in 1960, it remained empty until the Curzon cinema chain reopened it in 1967. Changing hands again in 1972, the auditorium was subdivided by Classic Cinemas with half of the former balcony becoming The Tatler Film Club, a small screen dedicated to showing uncensored pornography. Closing for good in 1981, the cinema was vacant until 1986 when it was converted to the Colindale Snooker Club. Still used for this purpose today, it's currently known as The Hurricane Rooms.

Though fairly intact, the faience clad façade isn't in great shape. The easily accessible nature of the design has left it open to vandalism and graffiti. The cheapest and simplest way of remedying this is to paint over each tag as it appears. Consequently, the once sharp tiled frontage is now a patchwork gallery of of different buff coloured emulsions, untouched faience, and fresh aerosol scrawls.

HURRICANE ROOM SNOOKER POOL BAR
LONDON CARS
TEL: 0208 200 5550
MINI CAB & COURIER SERVICES
SKASS FABRICS
HURRICANE ROOM
SNOOKER POOL BAR

O27 ISLEWORTH

484 London Road, Isleworth, TW7 4DH
1935 / George Coles

Without doubt, the Odeon that Coles designed for the west London suburb of Isleworth featured one of the most unusual cinema entrance halls of the period. It is perhaps even more surprising given that at this point Coles' practice was associated with a more ornate historical style of cinema exterior.

The tall oval building had a huge overhanging canopy which sat incongruently in front of the cinema's auditorium, which itself was tucked behind a row of shops constructed simultaneously. If unusual by day, by night its appearance was even more striking (see page 6). Rings of neon tubes illuminated the exterior, circling the futuristic structure in horizontal bands echoing the trend for 'nocturnal architecture,' popularised in Germany in the 1920s.

Alas, its time as a cinema was very short-lived, closing in 1957 due to falling attendances. The auditorium was gutted and converted into Isleworth Studios, a film production suite specialising in advertisements. This unusual diversification lasted until 2001. The following year, the former auditorium was demolished to make way for apartments. Thankfully, the original entrance building was retained and restored, to provide access to the flats, while the upper storey houses multiple businesses including Polish Radio London and Cooltura Magazine. These days, the building sits almost directly under the Heathrow flight path with descending aeroplanes regularly passing overhead.

ODEON PARADE
POLISH RADIO LONDON
cooltura

O30 BARNET

Barnet Hill, Barnet, EN5 1AB
1935 / Edgar J. Simmons
Grade II listed on 18 December 1989

The Barnet Odeon was bought from local operators County during construction. Externally, it was a near identical copy of County's 1932 cinema in Hertford (demolished in the 1980s). As such, it bears no resemblance to the emerging Odeon 'house style' that Weedon's office was developing at the time, but it is still an imposing Art Deco building with a striking North African lilt. Internally, there was just enough time to install a few Odeon touches, such as their usual geometric carpet and octagonal clocks, prior to the grand opening.

The cinema has had a virtually uninterrupted run screening films since 1935. In 1974, the grand auditorium was divided into three, with the primary screen in the former circle and two smaller ones in the rear stalls. Two more screens were added in 1992, utilising unused space in the front stalls and former stage areas.

In 2015, the relatively new independent chain Everyman bought out four Odeon cinemas, including Barnet. Following a substantial restoration, the cinema reopened in 2016 and has proved a resounding success with box office takings rising an average of 60%. Everyman chief executive Crispin Lilly explained that "we completely change the business model and can make these buildings work. There is nothing more satisfying than bringing an old cinema back to life."[1]

EVERYMAN
EVERYMAN
EVERYMAN

O31 WESTON-SUPER-MARE

18 Walliscote Road, Weston-super-Mare, BS23 1AA
1935 / Thomas Cecil Howitt
Grade II listed on 21 August 1986

At the time of publication, only eight original 1930s cinemas built by Odeon are still operated by the chain. While Leicester Square remains a jewel in the crown used for red carpet premieres and illustrious events, the others don't seem to be hold quite the same level of prestige. Of these, Thomas Cecil Howitt's glorious example at Weston-super-Mare should be considered the most important. Visually it built on the design cues developed for Howitt's Warley cinema in 1934 to stunning effect in a far more inventive form.

The auditorium was subdivided in 1973 following the tried and tested formula that the Rank Organisation was rolling out at the time; the rear stalls were partitioned to create a pair of small screens. A fourth screen was added in the former front stalls in 1991. Despite the internal alterations, the Historic England List entry highlights that "elements of the original layout of the cinema survive, including the upper part of the main auditorium, proscenium arch and main staircase, enabling the original design and main circulation spaces to be read. For its surviving internal decorative detailing and original fittings, which include a rare working example of an original Compton organ; understood to be one of only two examples known to survive in a functioning cinema."[2]

Controversially, despite both the listing and the cinema's continuing success in the popular coastal town, the local council granted permission for a huge multiplex to be constructed within walking distance of the Odeon. Opened in January 2018, the new eight screen Cineworld put an unwelcome question mark over the survival of its stylish elderly neighbour.

ODEON
ODEON
ODEON
FANATICAL ABOUT FILM

O32 KINGSTANDING

Kettlehouse Road, Birmingham, B44 9JD
1935 / John Cecil Clavering
Grade II listed on 10 October 1980

Though designed by Clavering via Weedon's office, this was not intended to be an Odeon. Commissioned by cinema-building newcomer B. G. Vale and due to be called The Beacon, the plans were ultimately sold to Deutsch with Vale becoming the manager instead. The site at a busy intersection of five roads in a rapidly expanding area of north Birmingham had previously been offered to Deutsch in 1932 but he didn't pursue it at the time.

Arguably one of the most important examples of English cinemas from the period, Clavering later admitted to being influenced by Granger & Leathart's magnificent Dreamland Cinema in Margate. Designed in 1933 — though only completed in 1935 — Dreamland was one of the first examples of a tall, narrow fin being used as both a focal point and a location for illuminated branding, with Clavering noting it was "the ideal emblem for a cinema"[3]. He later spoke of the trouble the central element had caused, suspending such a large mass directly over the entrance being a challenge from an engineering perspective. This contributed to the more practical asymmetric designs that followed.

Opened in July 1935, Kingstanding was only run as a cinema until 1962 when dwindling attendances prompted the Rank Organisation to transfer it to their Top Rank Bingo arm. In 1990, Rank bought out the Mecca Leisure Group and slowly converted all of their existing bingo clubs to the brand throughout the decade.

MECCA

O40 FAVERSHAM

9 Market Place, Faversham, ME13 7AG
1936 / Andrew Mather
Grade II listed on 22 March 1988

Though some of Deutsch's early cinemas dabbled in neo-traditional designs, Faversham was the first and only Odeon built that fully embraced a Tudorbethan appearance, given that the similar and equally impressive Salisbury Gaumont cinema was only rebranded as an Odeon decades after construction.

Situated on the cobbled streets of a historic Kent market town, this boutique cinema was designed by Mather specifically to blend in with its genuine sixteenth century neighbours. However, despite the impressive central lead flèche and handmade roof tiles, Faversham was a relatively cheap project for Odeon at the time compared to the grander venues simultaneously under construction.
If the exterior suggested a historical atmosphere, the interior certainly didn't disappoint. The small stadium style auditorium was clad in wooden panelling adorned with decorative plaster animals and flowers, whilst illumination was provided by lanterns hung from the arched ceiling. Happily, these features have been preserved.

Sold to Classic Cinemas in 1967, who promptly offloaded it to Coral two years later, it became the Royal Cinema in 1969. Alternating between bingo and films, it continued to trade until 1987 when it was closed. After one false start, it reopened under independent ownership as the New Royal Cinema in 1994. It continues to be a popular cinema, that is well supported by the community with an enviable stream of glowing reviews and five-star ratings online.

New
ROYAL
COUNTRY BRIDES

O41 CORBY

Rockingham Road, Corby, NN17 1AD
1936 / Laurence M. Gotch

In 1934, the small Northamptonshire town of Corby saw seismic change as the first blast furnace in the brand new Stewarts and Lloyd steel works was lit. Over the following three years, the site would mushroom, becoming a major producer of pig iron and steel tubes in both the national and international markets.

To attract and retain employees, the firm were keen to invest in the town and so entered into partnership with Deutsch to build a new Odeon cinema. Designed by Kettering architect Gotch who was working in London at the time, the cinema boasted a symmetrical façade of faience and brick, with rows of retail units running off from each corner.

The Odeon closed in 1969 and following a ten month spell run by an independent operator, became a bingo hall until 1991. The building then re-opened as a furniture showroom in 1996. Over the years the faience and brickwork have been lost to generic painted render, with blanked-out windows, a pitched roof and roller shutters added. Although still trading at when this photograph was taken, a planning application to demolish the building and construct apartments on the site was submitted to Corby Borough Council in March 2018. If the plan proceeds, only the façade will survive.

FURNITURE CLEARANCE OUTLET
FURNITURE OUTLET
FURNITURE CLEARANCE OUTLET
BEDS
MATTRESSES
BEDROOM
DINING
LIVING
SOFAS

O42 SCARBOROUGH

Westborough, Scarborough, YO11 1JW
1936 / John Cecil Clavering & Robert Bullivant
Grade II listed in 1988; subsequently de-listed

1936 was an important year for Weedon's practice as many of the designs that he and his team of young architects had been working on since partnering with Deutsch finally reached completion. Chester, St Austell, Colwyn Bay, and Sutton Coldfield were all important architectural milestones in the Odeon circuit, but the first to open – thanks to a trouble-free rapid construction – was Scarborough. Started by Clavering and completed by Bullivant, Scarborough was a triumph in cinema design with a streamline form clad in faience, brick, glass and neon. Its nocturnal presence was reinforced by nearby street architecture; a branded illuminated pylon with neon rings placed on an adjacent traffic island. Inside the cinema, there was an extremely decadent auditorium designed by Mollo & Egan, and a large restaurant behind the curved first storey glazing.

By the mid 1980s, this was the only surviving purpose-built Odeon left in the chain that hadn't been subdivided. In 1988, it was granted Grade II listed status. James Whittell, the chain's managing director at the time, recalled his frustration at the inability to get the council's permission to split the auditorium: "I presented them and English Heritage with a very sensitive tripling scheme which would have maintained the cinema in its existing glory. This was flatly turned down."[4] As a last resort, the cinema was closed later that year in the hopes that a new application to subdivide the auditorium would be approved to secure the future of the cinema. Planning permission was rejected once again.

To add insult to injury, within three years permission was granted to new owners to dramatically alter the interior, converting it for use as a theatre-in-the-round, with film screenings only in the former circle. However, the Stephen Joseph Theatre have proved extremely worthy custodians and continue to operate from the building, hosting an eclectic program of touring events and community groups.

CINEMA
THEATRE
SJT
STEPHEN
JOSEPH
THEATRE
THEATRE
THEATRE SJT.UK.COM CINEMA SHOP

O43 SUTTON COLDFIELD

Maney Corner, Sutton Coldfield, B72 1QL
1936 / John Cecil Clavering & Harry Weedon
Grade II listed on 18 November 1998

The Sutton Coldfield Odeon proved to be iconic and archetypal. The asymmetric Clavering design with slab tower, curved corner entrance, and a mixture of buff faience and brick cladding was so successful that it was recycled for Harrogate, modified for Newport, and was a clear influence in many other subsequent designs. Clavering later commented that it was – compared to his previous design at Kingstanding – "much more satisfactory" both aesthetically and structurally, as the tower "broke up the façade very nicely"[5] and was supported by the projection room staircase.

The exterior is still mostly original and in excellent condition. The Historic England List entry cites in particular the brickwork, noting "vertical brick ribbed decoration with horizontal bands at cornice level. The cinema is unusual in sustaining its interest through high quality brickwork on all elevations."[6] The only major feature to have been lost is the red 'CINEMA' fin protruding from the tower, still extant at its Harrogate counterpart. It had been removed by the 1960s, perhaps due to the aftereffects of damage sustained during the war.

Though not the first Odeon/Rank cinema to be 'tripled,' it was, in 1972, the first to use the 'drop wall' method by creating two small screens at the rear of the stalls under the circle. That method was subsequently rolled out to over 50 further cinemas in the group. A fourth screen was added in the former front stalls in 1987.

It was rebranded Empire Cinema following a buyout by Irish based Ward-Anderson Cinemas in March 2006.

EMPIRE
CINEMAS

O46 WELL HALL

99 Well Hall Road, Eltham, SE9 6DB
1936 / Horace Ward & Andrew Mather
Grade II listed on 8 February 1989
Note: the listing has not been altered to take the substantial changes into account

Designed by Horace Ward from within Mather's practice, Well Hall was an attractive cinema that neatly fitted neatly into the Odeon's emerging 'house style' without repeating anything seen in the circuit to date. The most notable external feature, apart from the sizable canopy, was the curved glazed tower encasing the stairwell to the balcony. This heavy use of glass had been a key element in European Modernist architecture for well over a decade but was far less common in English cinema design.

In 1981, the Rank Organisation sold the cinema, which had been subdivided eight years earlier, to Panton Films. The renamed Coronet cinema closed for good in 2000.

Despite various proposals to save the building in its original form, the auditorium was demolished in 2011. Contrary to popular opinion, not even its Grade II listed status was enough to save it. By 2015, a new gymnasium and fitness centre had been erected on the auditorium site, with the foyer serving as an entrance. As a consolation, the gym reception retains many of the original features, including the paybox and a beautiful Terrazzo floor with 'ODEON' inlayed in red and green.

INESIS
Gym & Fitness Centre
Fitness for the Mind, Body and Soul
BETFRED
Pizza Hut

O51 BRIDGWATER

Penel Orlieu, Bridgwater, TA6 3PA
1936 / Thomas Cecil Howitt

Following the resounding success of Weston-super-Mare, Thomas Cecil Howitt designed two further Odeons with similar traits. Opened just over a month apart in the summer of 1936, Bridgwater and Clacton-on-Sea echoed each other's appearance consisting of a series of rectangular sections clad in basket weave faience. They also both featured Howitt's trademark tower, with a large overhanging slab roof supported by a series of short pillars. In Bridgwater, the design also incorporated a row of retail units with accommodation above.

Bridgwater was sold to Classic cinemas in 1967. The new owners removed the flat roof from the tower soon after. The reason for this decapitation is not on record but we can surmise that the slab had become damaged and deemed unsafe. In 1973, the auditorium was subdivided to create a bingo hall in the stalls while two small screens were installed in the former circle. Operators have changed over the years but it continues in this format today.

The poor condition of the exterior led Sedgemoor Council to issue a compulsory repair order in 2016 mandating replacement of the boarded up windows and doors, repairs to the canopy and roof, removal of graffiti, and replacement of crumbling render before making good and repainting the exterior. Following a lack of action, the owner was fined. The building has since changed hands and discussions over its restoration continue. Despite its poor condition, it outlived its sister Odeon in Clacton-on-Sea which was demolished in 1984.

MECCA
Bingo
CINEMA
MECCA
MECCA
Bingo

O52 DEAL

32-36 Queen Street, Deal, CT14 6EY
1936 / Andrew Mather

Deal, on the Kent coast, was home to the first of several Mather designed Odeons to be clad in Vitrolite panels rather than faience tiles. The 'Colourful Structural Glass' was an American innovation developed around the turn of the century. These large sheets of opaque coloured glass were initially used as a more economical alternative to marble panels for work surfaces and wall coverings in bathrooms and kitchens, but by the inter-war years it was being used increasingly in commercial cladding.

The glossy panels were cheaper and quicker to apply than faience tiling, but arguably displayed less finesse. The Deal Odeon featured large plain expanses in peach with vertical black detailing and thin horizontal bands in green, all reinforced with neon. The horizontal bands continued down the high street onto a row of shops built concurrently.

The Rank Organisation sold the cinema to the Classic chain in 1967, who ran it for 20 years before an independent operator rebranded it Flicks. Since 2009, it has been used a nightclub under several different brands including Academy, Rivals, The Channel Club and, at the time of photographing, Ocean Rooms.

Sadly, the Vitrolite panels have long since been removed and the exterior currently sports an expanse of peeling magnolia paint.

THE POOL ROOM
AT OCEAN ROOMS
OCEAN ROOMS
OPEN AS USUAL
OCEAN ROOMS
OPEN AS USUAL

O53 SOUTHALL

58-78 High Street, Southall, UB1 3DB
1936 / George Coles

By the end of the 1930s, moviegoers in Southall were well catered for, with four substantial cinemas to choose from. They ranged from the stunningly futuristic Dominion by Frank Ernest Bromige to Coles' impressive Palace Cinema, designed in the form of a Chinese temple for United Picture Theatres Ltd. The last addition to the town's set was the Odeon, another Coles design, though in comparison, it was a far less adventurous offering than might have been expected.

Following its closure in February 1961, the Southall Odeon became one of the Rank Organisations early experiments in diversification, when it reopened as a ten pin Top Rank Bowl in August of that year. Failing to generate the revenue that Rank had predicted, the venue soon closed.

After a period of vacancy, MFI took on the building in 1970 and repurposed it as a furniture showroom. Today, the former stalls area houses a Lidl supermarket, while the upper storey is home to Queenstyle Furniture.

The Odeon brand name was moved to the former Palace – which had since been bought out by Gaumont – for the duration of the 1960s, until that too was sold off. Now Grade II* listed, it is used as an indoor market. Sadly, the Dominion cinema was demolished in 1982.

LIDL
P
LIDL
QUEENSTYLE
FURNITURE
FURNITURE SHOWROOM 2nd & 3rd FLOORS
www.qsfurniture.co.uk

O56 ASHFORD

33-37 High Street, Ashford, TN24 8TF
1936 / Andrew Mather

Ashford was home to one of the more obvious take-over builds, bought with planning permission already in place. Though designed by Mather as a Regal cinema, it bore none of the trademarks his practice utilised in direct commissions for Deutsch. The brick façade with reconstituted stone details was positively Neo-Georgian and more in line with the designs used by the rival Gaumont chain. The auditorium was large, set some way back from the foyer at a cantered angle.

The Rank Organisation converted the cinema to a bingo club in 1975. This operated until May 2018 when it closed.

Following closure, Ashford Borough Council made plans to demolish the building and replace it with a "predominantly residential development." Upset by the potential loss of the building and the opportunities that repurposing it could offer, a petition was started by local resident Diccon Spain, who stated "I was deeply saddened to discover that despite huge public demand, the A.B.C. leadership already seems to have set the direction for one of the final remaining development sites in the heart of the town for more residential development."[7] Following over 3000 signatures, the council reconsidered their position and began looking at the feasibility of converting it for use as a theatre. In February 2019, plans were unveiled to demolish part of the building, retain the façade, and create a 'multi-million pound leisure complex' incorporating an outdoor cinema, theatre, restaurants and residential dwellings. In Response, opponents of this plan have recently applied for listed status.

HSBC

O57 IPSWICH

Lloyds Avenue, Ipswich, IP1 3HT
1936 / George Coles

Although Weedon, Mather and Coles were credited with designing the bulk of the Odeon estate, they weren't necessarily the architects responsible for designing each concept. Weedon was widely known to have operated primarily in a managerial capacity, crediting each building's true author with the Assistant Architect role. Meanwhile, many of Mather's cinemas are said to have been designed by Thomas Braddock. Coles, however, was less meticulous in crediting where delegation occurred, though given the huge volume and vast range of styles coming from the practice, it's almost inevitable that multiple personalities were at work.

Opening two weeks after Southall, Ipswich was clearly from the same drawing-board, but as a corner plot it had to contend with two walls on public show rather than one. Many of the design details from Southall were recycled, though the overall form at Ipswich is the more successful of the two.

The cinema lived an uneventful life. Like many of its counterparts, it was 'tripled' in 1975 and then closed as a cinema in 1982. With the partitions removed, it became a Top Rank Bingo, and was later rebranded as Mecca Bingo.

In 1991, the Rank Organisation opened a new five screen Odeon in the town just a third of a mile away. Designed by the Renton Howard Wood Levin Partnership, it revived many 1930s streamline design cues whilst retaining a clear Post-Modern identity. The cinema did not prove to be a success; it closed just fourteen years later. Initially sold to a property developer, the building was unused for over a decade until 2018 when Hope Church bought the building and submitted plans to convert it into a place of worship.

MECCA Bingo
Welcome to Mecca Ipswich
NEARLY NITES
@MECCA
LIVE TRIBUTE SHOWS
ELTON JOHN
CLASSIC ROCK
ROBBIE WILLIAMS
NEARLYFESTIVAL.COM
JACKPOTS
MECCA
Bingo

O58 MUSWELL HILL

Fortis Green Road, London, N10 3HP
1936 / George Coles
Grade II listed on 6 March 1984
Upgraded to Grade II* on 19 September 1997

As the only former Odeon to receive Grade II* listing by Historic England, Muswell Hill is undoubtedly one of Coles' greatest achievements. Built as part of a mixed development with shops and flats above, the original 1935 design placed the cinema on the corner of the plot directly opposite St James' Church. Despite the concept gaining planning consent, the church was unhappy and lobbied the council to refuse the cinema a licence. Further revisions followed to simplify the cinema façade to a more Expressionist style and to reposition it further away at 90 degrees to the church. The new proposal was evidently more palatable, and the cinema opened the following year.

The Historic England List entry, granted in 1984 states that Muswell Hill has "the most elaborate interior of any Odeon cinema to survive. Because of the restrictions placed on the external façade, the opportunity was taken to make the interior more lavish than was usual in the Odeon circuit, and the result is an elegant design of unusual imagination and crispness."[8]

The auditorium was 'tripled' in 1974 by installing two small screens under the circle and decommissioning the seating in the front stalls. In 2015, the Everyman group bought four Odeons including Muswell Hill (see also the entry for Barnet), and refurbished the building. Controversially, despite the Grade II* listing, two further 'pod' screens were installed in the circle the following year. Meanwhile, the former stalls were brought back into use as seating for Screen 1, taking the screen count to five.

EVERYMAN
EVERYMAN
COLES HOUSE
107-143
LADY BIRD
THE SHAPE OF WATER
BLACK PANTHER

O61 BROMLEY

242 High Street, Bromley, BR1 1PG
1936 / George Coles

A substantial number of the early Odeons were built in England's South East; the affluent Kent town of Bromley was on Deutsch's radar from the outset. Securing a site was more troublesome than he hoped, by October 1933, a suitable plot opposite Bromley North Station had been found and Coles instructed to draw up a scheme. However, by the time the plans were passed it had become apparent that the rival Gaumont chain were also planning to build a large cinema in the town. Not one to be outdone by the competition, Deutsch abandoned the original site in favour of a more awkward plot in a central High Street location. Determined to maximize the impact of a very narrow entrance in a densely packed street, Deutsch turned down a set of classically detailed plans from Coles, demanding instead a more eye-catching up-to-date frontage. The ultimate design didn't disappoint.

Opened in September 1936, Odeon Bromley seated just under 1500 patrons, 1000 fewer than the Gaumont that opened two months later. Odeon continued to run the cinema until 2006, having 'tripled' the auditorium in 1976 and reconfigured the layout again in 1988. Empire Cinemas Ltd. ran it for the following decade before Cineworld took over. Closing in 2018 and transferring it to their boutique Picturehouse arm, the extremely tired building was treated to a major refurbishment inside and out. Speaking of the project, joint Managing Director Clare Binns said, "When you walk through the door you'll be welcomed with a wonderful blend of classic Art Deco design with modern Picturehouse touches. Bromley is set to become one of our most beautiful and romantic projects – it'll be a true cathedral of cinema."[9] The Bromley Picture House opened 7 June 2019.

BROMLEY PICTUREHOUSE
6 SCREENS
BAR & KITCHEN
BECOME A FOUNDER MEMBER TODAY
Picture house
Picture house
FOOD & FILM

O62 HARROGATE

East Parade, Harrogate, HG1 5LB
1936 / W. Calder Robson & Harry Weedon (& J. Cecil Clavering)
Grade II listed on 24 May 1988

The Harrogate Odeon was a near carbon copy of Clavering's design for Sutton Coldfield which had opened five months earlier. The only notable changes were some additional windows and a slightly larger auditorium, with 47 more seats over the two levels. Despite being essentially Clavering's design, Harrogate is credited to Robson and Weedon. Clavering had left the practice earlier in the year after being offered a more lucrative position at The Office of Works and being posted to Shanghai. Bullivant succeeded Clavering as the chief architect at Weedon's practice.

Like Sutton Coldfield, the auditorium was 'tripled' in 1972, then partitioned again in the 1980s to create four screens. Harrogate had a fifth screen added more recently by splitting the circle in two.

In 1996, The Royal Mail included an image of the cinema in a series of stamps released to celebrate 100 years of cinema, which is proclaimed on an information plaque on the building.

It is one of the few cinemas from this period still retained by Odeon, but since 2016 has had to compete with a brand new five screen Everyman cinema situated less than 100 meters away.

CINEMA
ODEON
ODEON
FANATICAL ABOUT FILM

O63 CHESTER

Northgate Street, Chester, CH1 2HQ
1936 / Robert Bullivant & Harry Weedon
Grade II listed on 7 February 1989

Chester was one of the more protracted Odeon builds; It certainly didn't run smoothly. Proposing to build within the historic city walls led to months of drawn out discussion and sketches before the Royal Fine Arts Commission gave consent in principle. Following this, architect Bullivant was forced to draft over twenty different plans before approval was finally granted. Notable concessions included eschewing the Odeon circuit's trademark faience tiles, and an all-capitals typeface replicating the lettering on Trajan's column in Rome instead of the Odeon's usual octagonal branding.

After approval was granted and work finally commenced, the build was halted for over two months due to discovery of Roman antiquities in the foundations. Ultimately, some of these treasures would be put on permanent display in an integrated glass cabinet in the upper foyer. It finally opened in October 1936. The auditorium was split into three in 1976, then the largest of the resulting screens was itself 'tripled' in 1991 for a total of five screens.

The cinema operated as an Odeon until its closure in 2007. Proposals for its reuse were put forward by various bodies. There was a huge level of public support to preserve not just the building, but also its use as a cinema. Ultimately, after five years sitting vacant, Chester City Council stepped in and bought the site and embarked on an extensive project to rejuvenate the structure. Opening in 2017 with dramatic alterations internally and a significant extension to the rear, The Storyhouse is now home to an 800 seat theatre, a 100 seat cinema, a library, a restaurant and bar, plus rooms for clubs and community groups to use for meetings and functions.

STORYHOUSE
MAMMA MIA! HERE WE GO AGAIN (PG)
6 July – 26 August
theatre
cinema
library

O64 STAFFORD

3 Newport Road, Stafford, ST16 2HH
1936 / Roland Satchwell

Roland Satchwell, both individually and as part of the Satchwell & Roberts partnership, was one of the most prolific British cinema architects of the period. Designing for independent operators and established chains alike, he is credited as being behind over 50 cinemas in the inter-way period. However compared to the innovative designs of many of his peers, Satchwell's work was less progressive and this could well be the reason behind his relatively unsuccessful partnership with Deutsch.

Of his first two Odeon designs, in Birmingham's Warley & Shirley suburbs, Deutsch had Thomas Cecil Howitt completely redesign the former in a much more striking Art Moderne style. Peterborough suffered a similar fate; with Harry Weedon revisited Satchwells drawings. It was in this context that Deutsch disparagingly nicknamed Satchwell's Stafford construction The Drawing Room due to its compact dimensions and bland aesthetics. Deutsch only commissioned Satchwell once more, for Hereford, which required a stone clad Neo-Classical façade to blend in with its historic surroundings.

In 1981, the Rank Organisation sold the Stafford Odeon to the Hutchinson Leisure Group who 'tripled' the auditorium. It was then taken over by Apollo in 1988, and Curzon in 2014. In early December 2017, Curzon unexpectedly announced that the cinema would close the following week. An independent operator, AJH Cinema, had a bash at running it from May 2018 but it closed again the following February. Any future film screenings at the site look unlikely since the opening of a brand new six screen Odeon LUXE cinema in the town in November 2018.

CINEMAS

O70 LOUGHBOROUGH

Baxter Gate, Loughborough, LE11 1TG
1936 / Arthur J. Price & Harry Weedon
Grade II listed on 17 December 2007

Situated just outside of the town centre, the original Loughborough Odeon bore a striking resemblance to another Weedon Partnership design, the independent Tower Cinema which opened in West Bromwich the previous year. Whilst the earlier cinema suffered dereliction and demolition, its East Midlands relative has led a comparatively sheltered life.

Run as an Odeon for 31 years, it was sold to the Classic chain of cinemas in 1967. Classic dabbled in a mixed programme of bingo and film, before selling it on two just years later for use as the Vogue Social Club. That was a short-lived venture and the venue returned to cinema use soon after, but ultimately became a full-time bingo hall in 1974.

December 2007 saw the structure granted Grade II listing by Historic England, who noted the well-preserved nature of the building both inside and out. The only real blight to the frontage, aside from stereotypically garish bingo graphics, is the unfortunate positioning of the air-conditioning units on the canopy.

Ironically, since 2011, Loughborough's former New Empire Cinema has been run by Odeon. Originally an Edwardian picture house, it was dramatically reworked with a Weedon style frontage by Archibald Hurley Robinson in 1936. It is a charming slice of Thirties Art Deco, albeit with a much more compact façade than its streamlined one-time competitor that was specifically designed for the Odeon roster.

BINGO
BEACON BINGO
BEACON BINGO
JK
JK TRANSPORT
2 MEALS
£6.99
CURRY

O71 PORTSMOUTH

94 London Road, Portsmouth, PO2 0SZ
1936 / Andrew Mather

Despite occupying a modest area on the street, Odeon Portsmouth was one of the largest and most expensive cinemas the chain had built to date. The frontage was only as wide as the monolithic slab that towered over the pavement, with separate retail units either side bridging the gap to the neighbouring buildings.

'Tripled' in 1973, and increased to four screens in 1990, the cinema continued to be operated as an Odeon until its closure in 2008. At the time of writing, the former foyer and neighbouring retail units have been merged and used for a Sainsbury's Local convenience store, while the partitioned auditorium was still standing, but unused. Recent urban explorer videos posted online expose the dire state of the former screens with severe water damage, vandalism and pigeon infestation dampening any hopes of future re-commissioning.

Originally clad in cream faience with green banding, the tower was painted white in the 1990s. This was a common and unwelcome fate for tiled frontages as it was a cheap and cheerful way of reducing maintenance and giving a short-term lift to the appearance.

Sainsbury's Local
Open Sunday to Thursday 8am - 9pm
Friday to Saturday 8am - 10pm
Sainsbury's Local
garbo's hair
UNSPUN
WITH MATT FORDE
TRUMP
PUTIN
Free cash
withdrawals
Frozen food
GREAT
PRICE

O73 SITTINGBOURNE

High Street, Sittingbourne, ME10 4PG
1937 / F. C. Mitchell

Given the number of different configurations and owners that Sittingbourne has had over the years, it's a wonder the building is still in use at all! Originally designed for the small A. E. Abrams chain in 1934, Odeon bought the project during construction.

This small Kent town already had two cinemas at the time, so the large 1593 capacity Odeon struggled to sell out screenings in the early years. Despite this, the Rank Organisation held onto it until 1967 when it was sold and converted into a bingo club. In the early 1970s, the restaurant and former circle were fitted out as cinemas, while the stalls continued as a bingo hall. Over the following decades it changed hands several times, becoming a Cannon, Picturedome and finally New Century Cinema. The screen in the former restaurant was closed in 2006, and a several planning applications to convert the building for other uses were submitted and refused. This led to a period of closure from 2009, but new owners and an upgrade of equipment saw it reopen in 2015. The cinema continues to screen films upstairs while Mecca Bingo operates below.

NEW CENTURY
MECCA
NEW CENTURY
M.E.C.C.A
Bingo

O76 YORK

Blossom Street,York, YO24 1AJ
1937 / Robert Bullivant & Harry Weedon
Grade II listed on 23 April 1981

Many of the hurdles that delayed the development and opening of Odeon Chester also affected York. Like Chester, the local authorities were extremely unhappy about the idea of a modern cinema being built within the historic city walls. Eventually a plot just outside the walls on Blossom Street was agreed on, but even then the council would only consider conservative schemes. The final design bore similarities to Chester with no faience tiling or octagonal branding, but this time a more intricate brickwork was approved with a pattern that varied in tone and featured decorative banding.

In 1998, Odeon introduced a new narrower font for their logo to replace the octagonal typeface that dated back to 1930. The remaining estate was slowly rebranded over the next few years, but the application to replace the Trajan signage in York was refused. Allegedly, Odeon threatened to close the cinema despite good attendances unless permission was granted, but it wasn't forthcoming. They finally pulled the plug in 2006, leaving the sign intact.

The independent Reel Cinemas group took over the building and renovated the interior. The auditorium that had been 'tripled' in 1972 was further subdivided increasing the screen count to five in 2010. The Everyman Media Group took over the reins in 2017, updating the interior to fit with their highly successfully up-market business model.

ODEON
EVERYMAN
BREAKS THE INTERNET PG DEC 1ST
PETERLOO 12 23 11

O77 HANLEY

Trinity Street, Hanley, ST1 5LA
1937 by Arthur J. Price & Harry Weedon

Built on the site of the Grand Theatre — designed by Frank Matcham in 1897 — that was destroyed by fire in 1932, the Hanley Odeon was a curious design, cleverly shoehorned into a tight corner plot. The auditorium was set at a right angle to the curved entrance building which boasted a slab tower capped with an ultra-narrow illuminated band of glass.

Though small, the well-proportioned frontage looked far more impressive when its neighbour was a single storey garage. The office block that replaced it dominates the street scene, diminishing the old cinema's wow factor somewhat.

Closed as a cinema in 1975, the building was ignominiously stripped of its lavish interior decoration and used for storage. A fire broke out in August 1982; thankfully, the structure was saved. Following a period of vacancy in the 1990s, it was resurrected as a nightclub, with a separate bar operating from the former foyer.

CHEEKY
clearway

O78 FOREST GATE

292-296 Romford Road, London, E7 9HD
1937 / Andrew Mather

Several cinemas that opened as Odeons, were already designed, or, in some cases, were under construction, when Deutsch bought the original owners out. Examples such as Barnet, Kingstanding and Swiss Cottage exhibited enough modern design elements to sit comfortably alongside the circuit style that the chain became known for. Forest Gate, however, does not. Though credited to Mather, its Portland Stone clad exterior bore little similarity to the rest of his output; it's likely to be a design inherited from another architect.

In April 1941, a parachute mine that destroyed the neighbouring ABC cinema also damaged the Odeon, forcing its closure. Emergency repairs took place over the summer and it reopened four months later.

After closing as a cinema in 1975, a false floor was extended from the circle to allow the stalls area to be used as a snooker club. Access was via a side door, as the foyer remained boarded up and the circle space dormant. Following the club's closure in 1994, the building was converted into a mosque and Muslim cultural centre. Externally, this involved a number of alterations, such as the long overdue removal of the original signage. Several sculpted reliefs depicting Pan were also chiselled off; the scars and OSB plasters were still visible at the time of writing. Metal canopies were also installed over the three windows, each capped with an Islamic crescent moon.

MINHAJ-UL-QURAN INTERNATIONAL LONDON
Mosque and Community Centre
MINHAJ BOOKSHOP
TUITION CENTRE
MATHS
ENGLISH
SCIENCE
PRIMARY, SECONDARY, GCSE, SATs, 11+
07412 011 519
TUITION CENTRE
ENGLISH CLASSES

O80 WREXHAM

Brook Street, Wrexham, LL13 7LH
1937 / Alexander Budge Reed & Harry Weedon

This fairly uncompromising design in Wrexham, Denbighshire was the first of five Odeons realised by Scottish architect Alexander Budge Reid (alongside Harry Weedon). Notable perhaps primarily for its enthusiastic use of faience with no fenestration whatsoever above canopy level, its appearance would have been enhanced in period by neon and a suitably large illuminated Odeon sign across the façade.

'Tripled' in 1972 but converted to a bingo hall just four years later, it remained in the Rank portfolio until 1999 when they moved to new premises. The building has since been used as a Hard Rock Café and Liquid nightclub and is currently run as ATIK, also a nightclub.

As a point of interest, this was the first of three purpose-built Odeons in Wrexham. After a twenty-year gap Rank returned with a new seven screen multiplex in 1997, which in turn was superseded by another purpose built eight screen complex opening in 2009.

ATIK

O83 YEOVIL

Court Ash, Yeovil, BA20 1HG
1937 / Alexander Budge Reed & Harry Weedon

Though distinctly different in size and form from Budge Reed's previous design at Wrexham, Yeovil continued the theme of large quantities of buff faience cladding with little else to lighten or punctuate the design. Built into a hill on the edge of the town, its sharp cubic form is almost fortress-like. The interior by Mollo & Egan was a masterpiece, utilising Holophane lighting and geometric plasterwork. Concave domes inset into the auditorium ceiling were coated in cellulose that reflected coloured lights projected onto them, creating an optical illusion to entrance the audience.

The Rank Organisation sold the cinema in 1967 and, like many others, it was 'tripled' and continued to change hands over the following decades. The last of five cinema operators, ABC, closed the doors in 2002. Following this, it was converted into The Old Cinema Bed & Sofa Store, a curious diversification that traded for 11 years before closing in 2015. Shortly after, St Margaret's Hospice reopened the premises as a two storey charity shop with café named The Old Cinema Home Store.

NOW SHOWING
HOME STORE
St.Margaret's
St. Margaret's
THE OLD CINEMA HOME STORE
St. Margaret's HOME STORE
DROP OFF POINT
CUSTOMER PARKING

O89 DUDLEY

22 Castle Hill, Dudley, DY1 4QQ
1937 / Alexander Budge Reed & Harry Weedon
Grade II listed on 5 October 2000

Fourth in the run of five designed by Budge Reid & Weedon, Dudley's former Odeon has weathered the last 80 years remarkably well. Standing on Castle Hill just outside the town centre, it formed part of a collection of devilishly modern structures built in the Black Country hub during the period. Directly opposite is Tecton Group's groundbreaking Zoological Gardens (1935-7). Standing proudly next door was 1936's Plaza cinema, which in turn was adjacent to the Hippodrome (rebuilt in 1938).

The Odeon lived a relatively uneventful life, standing up to stiff competition from the other cinemas in the town, several of which also ended up being operated by the Rank Organisation. Closing in February 1975, it was snapped up by the International Bible Students Association who saw the potential for using the undivided 1876 seat auditorium as a church.

After 25 years, a major refurbishment was required. It reopened in 2005 as an Assembly Hall of Jehovah's Witnesses. During this period, the building was granted Grade II listed status by Historic England.

In 2019, it is heartening to see the former Odeon cared for with such enthusiasm and respect. Both the building and the surrounding plot look as crisp and fresh as they would have in 1937.

O91 BOURNEMOUTH

10 Christchurch Road, Bournemouth, BH1 1AA
1937 / George Coles

The huge Coles scheme at Bournemouth proved troublesome to get off the ground. The popular coastal resort was already home to fourteen other cinemas when Odeon submitted proposals; despite the site being well away from the town centre, they faced strong opposition. Planning permission was refused several times in 1936, but following a successful publicity campaign and some concessions to appease the competition, consent was finally granted.

The structure was by far the largest Odeon had undertaken to date and represented an unusual concept in the Great Britain at the time. While it wasn't uncommon to include retail units with owner's accommodation above in a new cinema development, the scale of the Bournemouth plan set it apart. The structure consisted of a row of 18 shops and 45 flats.

The cinema opened before the flats were completed. John Maltby's photo of the development showed the completed Odeon façade with the opening film advertised on the canopy, while the giant steel construction frame extended out horizontally from either side.
The cinema closed in January 1974 and was converted into a bingo club.

BINGO
BINGO
Premier
SANDS 2
07968 313 744
BH14 'TAXI' VAN

O96 EXETER

Sidwell Street, Exeter, EX4 6PL
1937 / Robert Bullivant & Harry Weedon

The Odeon at Exeter could be considered a rather unimaginative cubic building, but Bullivant's original touches to the exterior created a remarkable vertical emphasis. Four bands of buff tiles reinforced with neon scaled beyond the full height of the frontage before curving back away from the street. An extravagant canopy of the same colour highlighted with more neon held four curved elements that aligned with the vertical bands. This, combined with the three full height windows illuminated from within, must looked remarkable when viewed by night.

Like many key cities in the UK, Exeter suffered significant bomb damage during World War II. Much of the surrounding area was devastated in a ferocious incendiary attack on 4 May 1942; it is remarkable that the cinema survived at all. The building was closed for emergency repairs. The most notable casualties on the façade were the vertical bands, which were ultimately capped off rather than being restored to their former glory. The canopy survived in slightly altered form but was replaced with the rather underwhelming current iteration in the 1960s. The auditorium was also modernised in the 1960s and then 'tripled' in 1972. In 1988, this was increased to four screens by partitioning the circle fully from the former front stalls. Happily, unlike most of its contemporaries, Exeter still operates as an Odeon cinema.

ODEON
TICKETS FROM £6.00
HAIR GEM'S

O97 PETERBOROUGH

46 Broadway, Peterborough, PE1 1RS
1937 / Roland Satchwell & Harry Weedon

The original design for Peterborough by Satchwell gained planning permission in October 1935. It's unclear if the project was then bought out by Odeon, or if Deutsch was simply unhappy with the plans, but Weedon revised the designs prior to construction. The resultant cinema was clad in buff faience tiles arranged in a basket weave pattern with two raised bands rising vertically to a small decorative parapet. 'Tripled' in the 1970s, the Rank Organisation continued to run the cinema until 1991 when it closed in the wake of stiff competition from a new eleven screen multiplex nearby. In the years prior to this, the decorative adornments and tiles were removed and the exterior rendered.

Having been vacant since its closure, local philanthropist and Pizza Express founder Peter Boizot bought the stricken building in 1997 and commissioned architect Tim Foster to reinvent the building. The original auditorium period features were restored. The frontage was transformed with the installation of a protruding glass pod, and the bare façade was clad in white and blue mosaic tiles. Reopened in 2001 as Broadway Theatre with a mixed program of events and screenings, the venue was initially a success.

In January 2009, following a break-in, fire erupted inside the venue. The damage was extensive and hopes of a swift repair were dashed when the insurers refused to pay out.

A new owner took charge in 2010 and the venue reopened the following year, but it's been a rocky road ever since, with financial difficulties, closures, and further changes of management. In March 2019, it was announced that the venue would be renamed The Peterborough New Theatre and run by Selladoor Worldwide who vowed to "produce and present quality, diverse, daring and dynamic work"[8] there.

BROADWAY

098 MORECAMBE

Euston Road, Morecambe, LA4 5LE
1937 / W. Calder Robson & Harry Weedon

From humble beginnings as a fishing village, Morecambe (originally known as Poulton-le-Sands) saw a rapid period of expansion in the second half of the nineteenth-century with the arrival of a railway, a deep water port, and numerous leisure attractions for holidaymakers. Though the port itself was short lived, the resort continued to flourish as a tourist destination well into the twentieth-century. With the opening of the world-class Streamline Moderne Midland Hotel in 1933, it became a magnet for the rich and famous.

Morecambe already had a number of cinemas by the time the Odeon opened in 1937, and its out-of-town location was less than ideal. Despite this, it was a popular cinema for a period, but by the late 1960s the town's star was starting to fade as holidaymakers increasingly travelled abroad. With attendances dwindling, the Rank Organisation sold the Odeon to Classic Cinemas in 1967, who ran it for nine years. Since then it has been put to retail use. It is currently home to a DIY store.

The building isn't listed and requires urgent attention if its future is to be secured. In 2014, the Modernist Britain website described its current condition: "The walkway and windows are boarded or covered over, the canopy has been lost and the entrance walls clad with board. A large structure has been constructed on the roof of the tower and extraneous rendering applied to sections of brickwork. The external condition of the former cinema is in a poor state of repair."[9]

1ST STOP D-I-Y
GARDENING & HARDWARE
Fitted BATHROOMS & KITCHENS
HOMEMAKERS 1ST STOP
HOMEMAKERS 1ST STOP KITCHEN, BATHROOM & BEDROOM WORLD
BATHROOMS
KITCHENS
BEDROOMS
TILES

O99 SWISS COTTAGE

96 Finchley Road, London, NW3 5EL
1937 / Basil Herring & Harry Weedon

Originally commissioned by small operator Eldorado, Odeon bought the project and tasked Basil Herring to modify Robert Cromie's design prior to construction. Although specifics are hard to track down, the indications are that the cinema's final exterior probably didn't deviate greatly from Cromie's original design. Certainly, the red brick cladding was a significant departure from the usual circuit style at the time.

Standing on the extremely busy Finchley Road in the north London district of South Hampstead, the Swiss Cottage Odeon is one of the seven original cinemas to still be run by the chain today. Despite numerous internal alterations over the years, the exterior remains basically unchanged save for the signage.

In the 1960s, in line with many others operated by Rank, the interior was modernised* (*read as – remove period features). The auditorium was subdivided into three screens in 1973, with further multiplexing in 1992 upping the screen-count to six. 2011 saw major changes with the creation of an I-MAX screen (ultra-high-resolution projection where viewers sit closer to the screen than in traditional formats). In 2017 most of the screens received new LUXE seating; handmade reclining leather seats with retractable trays. Speaking some months after the launch, General Manger Anthony Thompson said "Since reopening in December we've seen an overwhelming response from our guests who have all welcomed the luxury upgrades to their local cinema"[10].

ODEON
LUXE
IMAX

O100 WOLVERHAMPTON

Skinner Street, Wolverhampton, WV1 4LD
1937 / P. J. Price & Harry Weedon
Grade II listed on 5 October 2000

Compared to dramatic tales of planning and construction struggles, war-time catastrophes, and protracted fights for survival, the former Wolverhampton Odeon has had a fairly dull time of it. Opening in September 1937, Price's design was described as "a particularly successful essay in streamlined modernism"[11] with a stepped design incorporating black, cream, red & green faience tiling.

The cinema survived unaltered with a single screen until 1973, when, like many others, it was 'tripled.' In 1983, this building and a further five Odeons, were transferred to the bingo arm of the Rank Organisation. With the partitions removed, the venue re-opened as a Top Rank Bingo Club, later rebranded to Mecca Bingo. Closure finally came in 2007, with management citing the new law banning smoking in public places as the cause.

Following a change of ownership and restoration works, the building reopened as the Diamond Banqueting suite in 2009. It was billed as offering "modern facilities in elegant surroundings that are not often seen in the West Midlands, with state of the art lighting, a professional sound system, spacious dance floor, licensed bar and full air conditioning."[12]

DIAMOND
PHONE
01902 427810
DIAMOND BANQUETING SUITE

O101 WOOLWICH

John Wilson Street, London, SE18 6QJ
1937 / George Coles
Grade II listed on 31 December 1973

Arguably the impressive Odeon on the southern banks of the Thames in East London was Coles' most memorable design; given that there were already several cinemas in the area, including the brand new Granada directly opposite, it was perhaps necessary to make a bold statement.

The exterior was a masterclass in faience clad streamline design with virtually no windows at all. By night, the building was illuminated in neon tubes, both outlining the silhouette and highlighting the details.

Such was its importance that it was the first Odeon to be granted listed status in 1973, at a time when the preservation movement for this period of architecture was still in its infancy.

Despite a strong local campaign to save the cinema, the Rank Organisation closed it in October 1981. A collective of staff members approached Rank with a plan to lease the cinema and run it independently, but this proved unsuccessful. Following a two year gap, it was taken on by an independent operator and reopened as the Coronet Cinema in 1983. In 1990, the huge auditorium was split into two screens, but the former Odeon screened its last film in 1999.

2001 saw the building reopen as a church known as Gateway House. The owners, New Wine Church, have undertaken a great deal of work to restore the building and keep it in fine fettle.

NEW WINE CHURCH
2017
OVERFLOWING
ABUNDANCE
GATEWAY HOUSE
JOHN WILSON
STREET

O102 RHYL

Brighton Road, Rhyl, LL18 3HD
1937 / Robert Bullivant & Harry Weedon
Grade II listed on 4 January 1989

Construction of the Odeon in the Welsh coastal resort of Rhyl was one of the least straightforward projects the company had undertaken. Local operators Rhyl Entertainments already ran three cinemas in the town and were building a fourth nearby. Despite the potential oversupply, permission was granted on the basis that monopolies were not in the public interest.

Work commenced but was swiftly halted when it became apparent that the water table was tidal and higher than expected. The foundations were flooding twice daily, requiring extensive modifications to solve the problem before work could continue.

Rhyl was another fine execution of the Odeon circuit style and was recorded in the List entry as "an important example of Art Deco cinema design - possibly the best of its kind in Wales - which retains most of its original internal and external character and detail."[13]

Sold by the Rank Organisation in 1969, independent operator Hutchinson renamed it the Astra Cinema and 'tripled' the auditorium three years later. Soon after, the stalls were converted into a bingo hall while the smaller screens continued to show films. Changing hands again in the late 1980s, it became the Apollo cinema for a few years. In 1995, the original auditorium was restored solely for bingo.

APOLLO
BINGO
APOLLO BINGO

O103 LEICESTER SQUARE

26 Leicester Square, London, WC2H 7LQ
1937 / Andrew Mather, Thomas Braddock, Harry Weedon & Arthur J. Price

Odeon's 2116 seater flagship cinema in London's Leicester Square sprung from a unique arrangement to ensure that the design was truly a jewel in the company's crown; Weedon's office worked in collaboration with Mather's practice. A number of designs were presented by different partners, all adhering to a consensus that the appearance should be the complete opposite of the established buff faience tile clad norm. The final design is said to be primarily by Mather staff member Thomas Braddock, with Arthur J. Price contributing from Weedon's side.

The huge monolithic structure that emerged took seven months to build and cost four times that of other major Odeons built that year. Dressed in glorious polished black granite and outlined in neon, it was, and remains, an undeniably Modernist building. A giant 120ft tower – reduced from an original 150ft proposal in order to meet planning regulations – to the left bears the brand in both vertical and horizontal illuminated type, overlapping at the letter O.

The entrance originally featured twelve etched glass doors depicting dancing figures and animals, designed by British artist Bainbridge Copnell. Above them, an ingenious recessed events sign listed the current attractions in giant illuminated letters, each part of an alphabetic conveyor that could be regularly changed by staff members.

The auditorium featured leopard skin print seats and giant fibrous mouldings of flying ladies leaping in front of a sun, a trio of which were placed on each side of the screen to symbolise 'the miracle of light making film possible.'

In 1967, the cinema was updated as part of the Rank Organization's wide-ranging and much maligned Zing programme. This included changes to the exterior signage and canopy, plus the removal of the etched glass doors. Internally, the work was even more extensive with an almost total gutting of the auditorium, including the iconic flying ladies (though replicas were installed in 1998). It was noted that on the grand reopening in December, Queen Elizabeth II was most unimpressed, stating "It is not an improvement!"[14]

In 1990, Glyn Mellor designed five new small screens in a former exit alleyway of the cinema. The new complex, first called Odeon Mezzanine and then Studios, had a separate entrance to the main cinema, but was sympathetically clad in matching black granite.

The cinema was closed for much of 2018 for a muliti-million pound modernisation of facilities, sound and audio equipment. Externally, new lighting was installed to recreate the original neon illuminations. Easier access to the Studio screens through the foyer was facilitated, which also carved out space for Oscar's Bar and Café. Odeon went to great lengths to reintroduce and Art Deco theme and "blend the glamour of the original venue with state of the art luxury and technology,"[15] even fitting leopard print carpet in a nod to the original auditorium seating fabric.

MARVEL STUDIOS
AVENGERS
ENDGAME
THURSDAY APRIL 25
DISCOVER IT IN
DOLBY CINEMA
ODEON
DOLBY CINEMA
MARVEL STUDIOS
AVENGERS
ENDGAME
IN CINEMAS APRIL 25
Tickets now on sale
OSCAR'S CAFE
ODEON LUXE LEICESTER SQUARE HOME OF PREMIERES
LIMITLESS
OSCAR'S CAFÉ
OSCAR'S CAFÉ
OSCAR'S CAFÉ
OSCAR'S CAFÉ
NO DRINKS TO BE TAKEN FROM THE OUTSIDE SEATING AREA

O109 CHORLEY

Market Street, Chorley, PR7 1BD
1938 / P. J. Price & Harry Weedon

Bullivant was quoted as saying that Price was "an architects' architect. He did very little on the administrative side. He preferred to be on the drawing board and produced some very good work, but he hadn't got much ambition. He could have been made a partner if he carried on, but he wasn't interested. He just loved drawing and working on the board."[16]

One of two Odeons by P. J. Price & Weedon to be completed in 1938, there is little of note to say about Chorley. Opened in February 1938, it had to compete with the newly opened Plaza cinema which was larger, and a several established picture houses in the town. It was retained by the Rank Organisation until its closure in 1971. Following a two year gap it was repurposed as a bingo club, changing names over the years. At the time of writing, it was operated as Buzz Bingo.

PLAY BINGO
BUZZ Bingo
PLAY SLOTS
BUZZ Bingo
WIN UP TO £20,000 EVERYDAY
JOIN TODAY
SLOTS OPEN TIL LATE
JOIN TODAY

O112 NEWPORT

Clarence Place, Newport, NP19 7AB
1938 / Arthur J. Price & Harry Weedon
Grade II listed on 12 March 1999

The design in Newport was a successful reworking of the plans penned by Clavering for Sutton Coldfield two years earlier. Both had a low-level curved corner entrance, a slab tower, and faience clad wall. The most obvious external difference between the two designs is the greater use of brick in Newport, with piers giving a more substantial textured look to the overall appearance.

Operated by Odeon until closure in 1981, it remained vacant for the best part of 20 years. Somehow, the building avoided demolition. It was restored and reopened as the Newport City Live Arena in 2003, only to close again a short time after. Brief spells as a church and cinema museum followed before changing hands again.

2016 saw it launch in its current guise; The NEON (Newport Entertains Our Nation), a play on the old 'Oscar Entertains...' advertising acronym from the 1930s. A wide range of live events were bolstered by the resumption of cinematic activities in 2018, with a focus on cult classics and family favourites.

THE NEON
CONCERTS - SHOWS - EVENTS - CINEMA
WWW.THENEON.CO.UK

O114 ELTHAM HILL

Eltham Hill, London, SE9 5ED
1938 / Andrew Mather

Odeon Eltham Hill had a lot to live up to, given that its near neighbour was the Tudorbethan Art Deco mansion Eltham Palace. However, despite the prolific innovation of Mather's practice, it turned out to be one of its less dramatic designs, though was undoubtedly more striking in the 1930s than in the modern day. The large rectangular frontage was clad in granulated matt glass panels that solved the problem of glare caused by the glossy Vitrolite that Mather had previously used extensively. The upper section was cream and the lower part was black with a terracotta band at canopy level. Strips of neon reinforced the horizontal emphasis, while uplighters on top of the canopy illuminated the frontage.

Perhaps the most remarkable thing about Odeon Eltham Hill was that it was built at all, considering that a large, established Odeon was less than half a mile away in the Well Hall area of north Eltham. Odeon Eltham Hill ended up screening the less prestigious Gaumont release program after the chains merged, and in 1949 it was rebranded as one.

MECCA
20
ZONE
Car Park

O115 BALHAM

Balham Hill Road, London, SW12 9EA
1938 / George Coles

Described as Balham despite its South Clapham location, this was the last Odeon to be photographed by John Maltby. A payment dispute led to Maltby's relationship with Deutsch breaking down and Salisbury Photo press taking over the contract and documenting the final 25 Odeon cinemas opened before the war. Maltby's last work for the chain captured the beauty of Coles' vast symmetrical creation by both day and night, showcasing the dazzling neon tubes that reinforced its streamlined façade.

In May 1941, the cinema suffered significant bomb damage that destroyed the right-hand side of the frontage. Thankfully, the auditorium avoided a direct hit so, despite its bombed-out appearance, business was able to resume swiftly following minor repairs and a clean-up. Ultimately, the façade was restored to its original appearance with remarkable accuracy.

The Rank Organisation closed Balham's doors in September 1972 and the building remained empty for two years before reopening as the Liberty Cinema. After six years of operation with increasingly reduced opening hours, the cinema closed for good in 1980. Five years passed in which the building fell victim to vandalism before the auditorium was demolished to make way for a residential development. The foyer was converted for retail use, with Majestic Wine Warehouse currently operating from the site. In the 1990s, the upper storeys of the remaining structure were converted to residential use with the addition of further windows and balconies. The frontage would remain remarkably presentable if it were not blighted by transmitters and semi-permanent scaffolding clinging to the fin.

MAJESTIC wine warehouse

O118 LLANELLI

Station Road, Llanelli, SA13 1AH
1938 / P. J. Price & Harry Weedon
Grade II listed on 26 August 2009

The last of the Welsh Odeons to open in the decade, Llanelli was generally considered a bit of a backwater compared to Cardiff and the tourist hotspots of Rhyl & Colwyn Bay. This proved to be an advantage to Deutsch, offering him an opportunity to open in a sizable town where no major operator was trading.

Built on the site of an old working men's club, it stayed with the chain until 1967 when Classic Cinemas took over. 'Tripled' in the early 1970s, it ran for another few years before the local borough council took over. Keen to expand from purely cinematic use, the larger upstairs auditorium was modernised and adapted in 1984 to cater for live drama performances, with an additional entrance structure built onto the side of the building. Theatre Elli operated until 2012. Ironically, it closed in anticipation of competition from a brand new multiplex Odeon cinema opening in the town.

Now Grade II listed, it is owned by a community group of enthusiasts who are painstakingly restoring the venue back to its former glory with an admirable level of detail. The auditorium partitions have been removed and work is under way to create a luxury venue and bar called Calon Live.

THEATR
CANOLFAN
ADLONIANT
LLANELLI
Leisure Centre
Caerfyrddin
Carmarthen
A4214 (A484)

O120 HALIFAX

Broad Street, Halifax, HX1 1YA
1938 / George Coles

The Halifax site was originally bought in 1936 by film producer Nat Cohen and his business partner J. Rafter who were seeking to grow their small cinema estate. Coles, who had designed their Regal cinema in Kettering, was commissioned once again. The plans were approved in late 1936, but with concerns about market saturation, given that Halifax already had ten cinemas at the time, the venture was sold to the ever-ambitious Deutsch during construction.

The Odeon Halifax was a good example of how designs varied dramatically depending on the specification of the client. While modern in appearance, the frontage was unusual and the recessed cylindrical columns of glass bricks bore more of a resemblance to the Kettering design than anything Coles ever designed for a direct Odeon commission.

The Rank Organisation closed the cinema in 1975, converting it to a Top Rank Bingo club. As of 2019, it was still operating as a bingo hall, trading under the Mecca Bingo brand.

MECCA
Bingo
MECCA
Bingo
Premier Inn

O122 BRISTOL

Union Street, Bristol, BS1 2DS
1938 / Thomas Cecil Howitt

Bristol was the fifth and final cinema that Thomas Cecil Howitt designed for Odeon. Despite including some of his hallmarks, it had an unmistakably unique appearance thanks to its cylindrical glazed corner entrance. Like Odeon Bridgwater, it also featured an overhanging flat roof, which was removed at some point in the late 1960s or 1970s. Though less obvious here as no evidence of it remains, the effect is still detrimental to the overall balance of the exterior.

Most of the internal decoration was stripped out in 1967 as part of the Rank Organisation's Zing cinema modernisation program. Closing in 1983, the entire shell was gutted for a refit. Three new screens were added at a right angle to the original layout, with a new side entrance created for cinema access. The former foyer and stalls area were converted for retail use; first as a Mothercare baby goods shop and then, as at the time of writing, an H&M fashion store.

The building's central tower, with a modified appearance and extended vertical fins, retained Odeon branding until the turn of the Millennium. It has since been restored to its original form, minus the roof, although the signage is now relegated purely to the current cinema entrance.

The cinema's history is littered with more dramatic footnotes than most. Struck by a bomb in December 1940, it closed for a mere fortnight while repairs were made to the circle and roof. In 1946, the 33 year old General Manager Robert Parrington Jackson was found in his office having been shot dead during a screening of *The Light that Failed*. Reports, possibly apocryphal, suggest that the gunshots were masked by the action on screen which also involved a shooting. Without a motive or a suspect, the crime remained unsolved until the assailant's deathbed confession over 40 years later, describing a failed robbery.[17]

ODEON
H&M
H&M
SALE
SALE

O123 EAST HAM

7 Barking Road, London, E6 1PW
1938 / Keith P. Roberts & Andrew Mather

Though perhaps not as eye-catching or evocative of the 1930s as other examples in the Odeon circuit. Roberts' design for the exterior of East Ham was well ahead of its time. In Britain, this type of simple rectangular frontage adorned primarily with glass is more commonly associated with post-war architecture. Given the flamboyant nature of the Edwardian Boleyn Electric Cinema that it replaced, and the streamline styling of the Granada Cinema (1936) just up the road, the Odeon was a bold, uncompromising statement of modernity.

Despite the relatively modest frontage, the auditorium had a sizable capacity of 2212. Somehow, it survived without subdivision until its closure in 1981. After laying vacant for 14 years it was bought by an independent operator who split the space into three screens. The Boleyn Cinema opened in 1995, specialising in Bollywood films. In 2014, it closed for further reconfiguration; the original stalls were converted to a banqueting suite, while the circle was subdivided into a two screen cinema.

BOLEYN CINEMA
ATR TAXACCOUNTANTS LTD
TEL:0207 998 0725
Lebara play
Boleyn Banquetting Suite
BOLEYN

O125 LEICESTER

Rutland Street, Leicester, LE1 1SA
1938 / Robert Bullivant & Harry Weedon
Grade II listed on 27 August 1997

Planning permission for the Leicester Odeon was applied for in 1936 and despite receiving some negative comments from the committee regarding its "plain and bare"[18] appearance, approval was forthcoming in October of that year. However, construction was put on hold due to concerns over the location, situated outside of the central shopping area. It ultimately proved impossible to find a better plot that was big enough to build a 2000+-plus seater 'Super Cinema' so, after a protracted search, work commenced on the original site.

Opened in July 1938, Odeon operated the cinema until July 1997. Even though it had been subdivided to four screens, a new purpose-built multiplex was constructed outside of the town and the Odeon brand moved. Grade II listing was secured a month after closure.

A period of vacancy followed until it was restored to a single space and reopened as The Athena Conference Centre and Banqueting Suite in 2005. 13 years on, it's in admirably well-kept condition and hosts regular public and private events, including live music, comedy, weddings, conferences, and themed evenings.

ATHENA
QUEEN STREET

O126 AYR

10 Burns Statue Square, Ayr, KA7 1UP
1938 / Thomas Braddock & Andrew Mather

The second half of 1938 saw several significant events for the Mather practice. In July, the first of three Odeons in Scotland would open in the coastal county town of Ayr, with two further examples in Motherwell & Hamilton following before the year was out. Sadly, Mather himself would not live to see these completed, as he passed away on November 4 following a long illness. The practice continued for a number of years under the leadership of Leonard Allen.

All three Odeons were built on a tight budget compared to their southern siblings, though still made a statement given the relative scarcity of moderne architecture in Scotland at the time; the country had been in economic decline since World War 1, and only started to recover in the second half of the 1930s.

Odeon Ayr, with its monolithic slab over the entrance, bore some similarities to Mather's design for Portsmouth, though was more pared back in this instance with a simple buff faience cladding detailed with vertical grooves.

Still operated by Odeon, the auditorium was 'tripled' in 1987 and increased to four in 1992.

Recently, local newspaper The Daily Record reported on talks between the council and the chain to relocate into the Kyle Centre as part of a £10 million revamp of the town's shopping centre. Planning was approved for construction of the cinema in 2015, though work has yet to commence. Odeon management has not commented on the proposal publicly, except to say "we're very proud of our fantastic cinema in Ayr, and we look forward to continuing to bring the latest and best entertainment to our loyal guests for many more years to come."[19]

ODEON

O128 LUTON

127 Dunstable Road, Luton, LU1 1BW
1938 / Keith P. Roberts & Andrew Mather
Grade II listed on 11 March 1999

Opening just three days before rival ABC's Savoy Cinema, which was in a more central location, the Luton Odeon was another sharp Modernist offering from Roberts.

Roberts, an assistant in Mather's practice, was responsible for five Odeons completed in 1938 and a further four the following year. Praised in the 1999 Historic England List entry as "a remarkably sophisticated piece of purist geometry, entirely lacking historicist references or Art Deco styling,"[20] Luton was another clear signpost of the direction that modern British architecture would have taken in the 1940s if war had not intervened.

The auditorium was 'tripled' in 1974 but it closed as a cinema just nine years later. With the partitions removed, it reopened as a Top Rank Bingo hall in July 1983.

Controversy struck the building in 1997 when the Rank Organisation rebranded the club as Mecca Bingo. Luton's sizable Muslim community was outraged, stating "it was an insult to Islam for the name of their holiest city to be associated with gambling."[21] On Christmas Day, protesters threw bricks through the old cinema's windows. Management subsequently agreed to remove the signage, leaving only the word 'bingo' on the external branding. Despite this concession, the club only survived another 12 months before closure. Since 2001 it has been The Cavalry Church of God in Christ or COGIC for short.

Regrettably, of Roberts' nine Odeons, only Luton and East Ham now remain standing.

COGIC
CALVARY CHURCH OF GOD IN CHRIST
WWW.COGICHQ.CO.UK - U.K Headquarters - T. 01582 877070

O137 BLACKPOOL

5 Dickinson Road, Blackpool, FY1 2AX
1939 / W. Calder Robson & Harry Weedon
Grade II listed on 11 March 1994

Reminiscent of the design used in Leicester Square, but clad with buff faience tiles rather than granite, Blackpool was the largest cinema that Odeon constructed in the period. Despite being chosen over a rival proposal by T. Cecil Howitt, it's fair to say that Calder Robson's offering wasn't exactly an imaginative design. Still, what it lacked in finesse, it made up for in sheer scale, seating over 3,000 people in its original single auditorium configuration.

The space was subdivided into three in 1975, but with a less invasive configuration than used elsewhere. The auditorium was so large that two smaller screens could be installed in the rear of the stalls without breaching the front of the balcony. Thus, when seated in the circle, the subdivision remained concealed. This format continued until closure in 1998, with blockbuster film releases still able to fill the 1300 capacity of Screen One.

After sitting vacant for several years, the building was taken over by Pink Leisure, who opened a gay bar and drag-cabaret theatre called Funny Girls in the space. The venue is extremely popular, and to quote one happy punter on a cinema forum: "This building looks better today than it probably has done in the last 20 years. All thanks to the pink pound."[22]

FUNNY GIRLS
FUNNY GIRLS
Funny Girls

O141 WORCESTER

Foregate Street, Worcester, WR1 1DX
1939-50 / Robert Bullivant & Harry Weedon

This plot was one of Deutsch's early acquisitions, purchased in 1929. Quite why it took so long to realise the construction of a new cinema is a mystery, but opening of a brand new Gaumont cinema almost directly opposite in 1935 finally spurred Deutsch into action. Operating the existing Silver Cinema as an Odeon was no longer sufficient. By 1937, plans had been submitted to construct a new cinema on an enlarged site.

Demolition took place in 1939, but by the time the shell was constructed the country was at war, so all work was halted. In late 1940, work recommenced with the installation of seats, but ceased again when a rival cinema owner publicly called for the fitters to be transferred to the war effort.

Following a Government survey, the site was deemed suitable for the storage of munitions and was requisitioned by the Ministry of Works. A side wall was removed to aid access and the auditorium became a holding facility for 'alloys in transit.'
In 1948, the site was repatriated to Odeon and the interior fitment was completed, albeit with a much more austere scheme than originally envisaged, for a January 1950 opening.

In 1974, as part of a swift refit, the auditorium was split into three screens. 1990 saw the front stalls area partitioned to accommodate a further two screens, and in 1997 the screen count was increased to seven by adding two more on the rear of the former balcony.

ODEON
COSTA
TO LET
harrislamb
01905 22666
modus
Sales
Lettings
LUNCH DEAL

O142 SAINT HELIER

Bath Street, Saint Helier, JE2 4SU
1952 / T. P. Bennett
Listed as 'Site of Special Scientific Interest' in 2001

During and after the war, building materials in the UK were rationed as hospital, school and house building was prioritised by the Government. Construction required a Ministry of Works licence and cinemas were, understandably, classed as low priority. As a result, the English Odeon's in the early stages of construction in 1939 wouldn't be completed until the middle of the 1950s. Despite suffering tremendously under German occupation during the war, and being afflicted by the same labour and material shortages, the Channel Islands weren't subject to the same post-war building controls. The Rank Organisation seized the opportunity to build the only completely new Odeon the decade would see.

The task to design the new cinema fell to T. P. Bennet & Son, the firm responsible for designing the Odeons at Highgate and Haverstock Hill. Situated some distance away from the town centre, planners insisted on the entrance being located on a new side road. Externally, the cinema bore many pre-war design cues. Curved corners, a tower, vertical branding, and a glazed corridor along the top of the frontage could all be traced to earlier Odeons. The cladding was more unusual, however, featuring a chequerboard pattern more reminiscent of Lutyens' inter-war social housing in Pimlico than of the Odeon circuit style. Internally, the decoration had more of a 1950s Festival of Britain flavour, with pre-war extravagancies exchanged for a more minimal mid-century simplicity.

The cinema continued to be run by Odeon until 2004, with the auditorium 'twinned' in 1980, 'tripled' in 1989 and 'quadrupled' in 1992. An independent operator screened films for five years as the Forum Cinema before the building was closed in 2009. Demolition was proposed, but since 2014 an evangelical group has called it home, open daily as the Freedom Church.

freedom
church
Church meets here

O145 SHEFFIELD

Flat Street, Sheffield, S1 1NN
1939-56 / W. Calder Robson, Robert Bullivant & Harry Weedon

When war was declared in September 1939, Odeon had four cinemas at different stages of construction. Worcester had been completed externally, while those in Westbourne Grove and Highgate were partially built. Despite planning permission being granted in 1937, only the steel frame had been erected on the Sheffield site before work was halted. Post-war building restrictions resulted in 15 years passing before work recommenced. It seems fitting that this skeletal steel frame was a long standing feature on the streets of Sheffield – 'Steel City' – rather than anywhere else!

In 1955, Bullivant revisited Calder Robson's original plans, modifying them for the new age. The original design featured a similar footprint to the front, but housed many more pre-war Odeon archetypal features, including a rounded entrance block, faience tile cladding, and a tall central fin reaching skywards. The original plans also extended further to the rear, incorporating office and retail space. Bullivant's redrawn plans retained only the cinema element, replacing lavish 1930s touches with a sharp mid-century modern shell. Much of the steel frame was removed and reconfigured into the new design, which finally opened in July 1956.

Sadly, Odeon Sheffield was under construction for longer that it operated as a cinema. After only 15 years, the space was converted for use as a bingo hall, which it remains today.

Mega Value
Play Bingo
£3.50
MECCA
Bingo
12 31 50 71
3 23 41 64 88
16 33 53
6 28 76
42 65 90
17 38 57 79
Book a party with us
MECCA
Bingo

A DEFINITIVE LIST OF CINEMAS BUILT BY OSCAR DEUTSCH/ODEON (1928 - 1970)

Chronologically listed by opening date

- Demolished
- Elements Remain
- Survive

Location	Architect(s)	Opened	Closed as Cinema	Demolished / Current Use
1928				
1 Brierley Hill	Stanley A. Griffiths	1 October 1928	25 July 1959	circa 1959
1930				
2 Perry Barr	Stanley A. Griffiths, Horace G Bradley	4 August 1930	3 May 1969	Banqueting Suite
1931				
3 Alfreton	Harry Clayton	16 April 1931	30 May 1964	1965
1933				
4 Weymouth	Harry Clayton	2 June 1933	31 October 1999	2004
5 Kingston	Adamson, Marshall & Tweedy	3 July 1933	9th August 1987	1989
6 Canterbury	Alfred & Vincent Burr	5 August 1933	17 October 1981	2009
7 South Harrow	A. P. Starkey	4 September 1933	12 February 1972	c1972
8 Lancing	Unknown	3 October 1933	20 January 1952	Mixed
1934				
9 Worcester Park	Yates, Cook & Darbyshire	8 January 1934	29 September 1956	1998
10 Tolworth	Yates, Cook & Darbyshire	9 January 1934	10 October 1959	1961
11 Kemp Town	Andrew Mather	1 February 1934	5 November 1960	1986
12 Worthing	Whinney, Son & Austin Hall	24 March 1934	27 September 1986	1987
13 Weybridge	A. P. Starkey	9 April 1934	31 December 1960	Unknown
14 Surbiton	Joseph Hill	14 April 1934	8 February 1975	1999
15 Wallington	Yates, Cook & Darbyshire	26 May 1934	27 April 1957	1960/Public House
16 Kingsbury	Arthur Percival Starkey	30 May 1934	9 September 1972	1972
17 Lewes	Andrew Mather	2 June 1934	2 October 1971	1982
18 Bognor Regis	Whinney, Son & Austin Hall	14 July 1934	16 November 1974	Bingo
19 Haverstock Hill	T. P. Bennett & Son	29 September 1934	23 September 1972	1972
20 Wealdstone	A. P. Starkey	15 October 1934	4 March 1961	1970
21 Blackheath	Stanley A Griffiths	20 October 1934	9 November 1960	1984
22 Welling	George Coles	22 October 1934	22 October 1960	Church
23 Cleveleys	George Tonge	24 November 1934	7 January 1961	2010
24 Warley	Clavering, Howitt, Satchwell, Roberts	22 December 1934	29 April 1970	1973
1935				
25 Colindale	A. P. Starkey	28 January 1935	4 July 1981	Snooker Club
26 Kenton	George Coles	11 March 1935	25 March 1961	1961
27 Isleworth	George Coles	20 March 1935	5 January 1957	2001/Offices
28 Shirley	Roland Satchwell	15 April 1935	29 October 1977	1985

Location	Architect(s)	Opened	Closed as Cinema	Demolished / Current Use
29 Guildford	Andrew Mather, J. Rawsworth Hill	13 May 1935	8 December 1996	2002
30 Barnet	Edgar J. Simmons	15 May 1935	-	Cinema
31 Weston-super-Mare	Thomas Cecil Howitt	25 May 1935	-	Cinema
32 Kingstanding	John Cecil Clavering	22 July 1935	1 December 1962	Bingo
33 Chingford	Andrew Mather	9 September 1935	3 June 1972	c1972
34 Sudbury Town	A. P. Starkey	16 September 1935	27 October 1956	Unknown
35 North Finchley	A. P. Starkey, Frederick Adkins	14 October 1935	26 December 1964	2013
36 Southgate	Bertie Crewe	16 October 1935	2 January 1981	1982
37 Sidcup	A. P. Starkey	21 October 1935	14 January 1961	2015
1936				
38 Rickmansworth	Andrew Mather	29 January 1936	5 January 1957	1965
39 Newton Abbot	Howard Williams	17 February 1936	1 July 1971	1983
40 Faversham	Andrew Mather	9th March 1936	1st May 1974	Cinema
41 Corby	Laurence M. Gotch	16 March 1936	1969	Furniture Showroom
42 Scarborough	R. Bullivant, H. Weedon, J. Clavering	28 March 1936	-	Cinema & Theatre
43 Sutton Coldfield	W. Calder Robson, H. Weedon	18 April 1936	-	Cinema
44 Wimbledon	Yates, Cook & Darbyshire	20 April 1936	26 November 1960	1960
45 Colwyn Bay	J. Clavering, H. Weedon	25 April 1936	10 October 1986	1987
46 Well Hall	Andrew Mather, Horace Ward	20 May 1936	13 January 2000	2011/Gym
47 Littlehampton	Andrew Mather	23 May 1936	1 June 1974	1984
48 Clacton-on-Sea	Thomas Cecil Howitt	30 May 1936	20 November 1980	1984
49 Guide Bridge	F. E. Drury, J. G. Gomersall	29 June 1936	11 March 1961	Church (unrecognisable)
50 St Austell	P. J. Price, H. Weedon	11 July 1936	23 August 2007	2007
51 Bridgwater	Thomas Cecil Howitt	13 July 1936	-	Cinema & Bingo
52 Deal	Andrew Mather	25 July 1936	29 November 2007	Nightclub
53 Southall	George Coles	17 August 1936	25 February 1961	Retail
54 Oldham	H. Weedon	19 August 1936	29 October 1983	1992
55 Ramsgate	Andrew Mather	22 August 1936	17 October 1985	1988
56 Ashford	Andrew Mather	31 August 1936	30 August 1975	Vacant
57 Ipswich	George Coles	7 September 1936	3rd July 1982	Bingo
58 Muswell Hill	George Coles	9 September 1936	-	Cinema
59 Cardiff	William S. Wort	14 September 1936	16 May 2000	2003/Retail (unrecognisable)
60 Kettering	H. Weedon	19 September 1936	29 October 1960	1974
61 Bromley	George Coles	21 September 1936	-	Cinema
62 Harrogate	W. Calder Robson, H. Weedon	28 September 1936	-	Cinema
63 Chester	Robert Bullivant, H. Weedon	3 October 1936	-	Cinema & Theatre
64 Stafford	Roland Satchwell	5 October 1936	-	Cinema
65 Horsham	George Coles	7 October 1936	10 January 1976	1981
66 Newport	Andrew Mather	17 October 1936	18 December 1982	1984
67 Herne Bay	Andrew Mather	2 November 1936	8 October 1987	1988
68 Lancaster	W. Calder Robson, H. Weedon	7 November 1936	1 February 2007	2010
69 Bury	P. J. Price, H. Weedon	16 November 1936	24 October 1981	2013
70 Loughborough	A. J. Price, H. Weedon	21 November 1936	12 January 1974	Bingo
71 Portsmouth	Andrew Mather	14 December 1936	10 January 2008	Retail
72 Falmouth	P. J. Price, H. Weedon	17 December 1936	3 May 1970	1976
Northwood Hills	A. Douglas Clare, Andrew Mather	28 December 1936	22 September 1973	c1973 Sold prior to opening

Location	Architect(s)	Opened	Closed as Cinema	Demolished / Current Use
1937				
73 Sittingbourne	F. C. Mitchell	4 January 1937		Cinema & Bingo
74 Warrington	Drury & Gomersall	11 January 1937	28 August 1994	1998
75 Lowestoft	Andrew Mather	23 January 1937	25 April 1979	c1979
76 York	Robert Bullivant, H. Weedon	1 February 1937	-	Cinema
77 Hanley	Arthur J Price, H. Weedon	13 February 1938	15 November 1975	Nightclub
78 Forest Gate	Andrew Mather	1 March 1937	31 October 1975	Muslim Cultural Centre
79 Reading	A. P. Starkey, Frederick Adkins	8 March 1937	25 November 1999	2002
80 Wrexham	Alexander Budge Reed, H. Weedon	13 March 1937	15 May 1976	Nightclub & Café
81 Hereford	Roland Satchwell	17 April 1937	1 March 1984	1985
82 Epsom	Whinney, Son & Austin Hall	19 April 1937	19 June 1971	1971
83 Yeovil	Alexander Budge Reed, H. Weedon	10 May 1937	1 April 2002	Shop
84 Aylsbury	Andrew Mather	21 June 1937	30 October 1999	2017
85 Bury St Edmonds	George Coles	5 July 1937	30 October 1982	1983
86 Harlesden	Whinney, Son & Austin Hall	12 July 1937	15 April 1972	1989
87 Crewe	Alexander Budge Reed, H. Weedon	26 July 1937	26 May 1983	1983
88 South Norwood	Andrew Mather	26 July 1937	20 February 1971	1971
89 Dudley	Alexander Budge Reed, H. Weedon	28 July 1937	22 February 1975	Church
90 Penge	Andrew Mather	31 July 1937	4 September 1976	1994
91 Bournemouth	George Coles	7 August 1937	16 January 1974	Bingo
92 Radcliffe	W. Calder Robson, H. Weedon	14 August 1937	27 April 1957	2005
93 Boston	Alexander Budge Reed, H. Weedon	18 August 1937	15 May 1987	1999
94 Bolton	W. Calder Robson, H. Weedon	21 August 1937	8 January 1983	2007
95 Burnley	Robert Bullivant, H. Weedon	28 August 1937	17 November 1973	2005
96 Exeter	Robert Bullivant, H. Weedon	30 August 1937	-	Cinema
97 Peterborough	Roland Satchwell, H. Weedon	2 September 1937	1 November 1991	Theatre
98 Morecambe	W. Calder Robson, H. Weedon	2 September 1937	28 February 1976	Retail
99 Swiss Cottage	Basil Herring, H. Weedon	4 September 1937		Cinema
100 Wolverhampton	P. J. Price, H. Weedon	11 September 1937	4 June 1983	Banqueting Suite
101 Woolwich	George Coles	25 October 1937	6 June 1999	Church
102 Rhyl	Robert Bullivant, H. Weedon	30 October 1937	-	Bingo
103 Leicester Square	Andrew Mather, H. Weedon	2 November 1937	-	Cinema
104 Acton	George Coles	8 November 1937	8 October 1975	1988
105 Edgeware Rd	George Coles	9 November 1937	7 June 1975	1990/1994
North Watford	J. Owen Bond & Son	27 November 1937	30 May 1959	1989 Sold prior to completio
106 Southsea	Andrew Mather	4 December 1937	1 September 1983	1985
107 Brighton	Andrew Mather	18 December 1937	19 April 1973	1990
1938				
108 Norwich	Basil Herring, H. Weedon	7 February 1938	26 June 1971	1971
109 Chorley	P. J. Price, H. Weedon	21 February 1938	6 February 1971	Bingo
110 Erith	George Coles	26 February 1938	25 September 1976	2002
111 Spalding	Basil Herring, H. Weedon	28 February 1938	1 July 1983	1987
112 Newport	Arthur J Price, H. Weedon	12 March 1938	30 May 1981	Events Venue
113 Kingswood (Bristol)	Frederick Charles Mitchell	26 March 1938	11 March 1961	1970
114 Eltham Hill	Andrew Mather	14 April 1938	19 June 1967	Bingo
115 Balham	George Coles	16 April 1938	1980	1985/Flats
116 Brentwood	George Coles	18 May 1938	20 April 1974	1974
117 Redhill	Keith P. Roberts, Andrew Mather	23 May 1938	18 October 1975	2013
118 Llanelli	P. J. Price, H. Weedon	18 June 1938	13 July 2012	Events Venue
119 Uxbridge	Andrew Mather	20 June 1938	5 June 1982	1984
120 Halifax	George Coles	27 June 1938	18 October 1975	Bingo

Location	Architect(s)	Opened	Closed as Cinema	Demolished / Current Use
121 Peckham	Andrew Mather	1 June 1938	1 December 1983	1985
122 Bristol	Thomas Cecil Howitt	16 July 1938	-	Cinema & Retail
123 East Ham	Keith P. Roberts, Andrew Mather	18 July 1938	-	Cinema & Banqueting
124 Hackney Road	Keith P. Roberts, Andrew Mather	27 July 1938	20 May 1961	2018
125 Leicester	Robert Bullivant, H. Weedon	28 July 1938	16 July 1997	Conference Centre
126 Ayr	Thomas Braddock, Andrew Mather	30 July 1938		Cinema
127 Deptford	George Coles	3 October 1938	16 May 1970	1988
128 Luton	Keith P. Roberts, Andrew Mather	12 October 1938	4 June 1983	Church
129 Mile End	Keith P. Roberts, Andrew Mather	17 October 1938	17 June 1972	1984
130 Shannon Corner	George Coles	7 November 1938	2 January 1960	1985
131 Hamilton	Andrew Mather	14 November 1938	26 August 1999	1999
132 Motherwell	Andrew Mather	3 December 1938	25 October 1975	1996
133 Bradford	Harry Weedon, Robert Bullivant	17 December 1938	22 March 1969	1969
1939				
134 Middlesborough	W. Calder Robson, H. Weedon	25 February 1939	24 June 2001	2006
135 Camberwell	Keith P. Roberts, Andrew Mather	20 March 1939	5 July 1975	1993
136 Dalston	Andrew Mather	1 May 1939	31 March 1979	1984
137 Blackpool	W. Calder Robson, H. Weedon	6 May 1939	1 January 1998	Cabaret Club
138 Canning Town	Keith P. Roberts, Andrew Mather	25 May 1939	11 May 1941	1970
139 Elmers End	Keith P. Roberts, Andrew Mather	26 August 1939	5 January 1957	c1957
140 Hendon	Robert Bullivant, H. Weedon	28 August 1939	13 January 1979	1981
1950s - under The Rank Organisation ownership				
141 Worcester	Robert Bullivant, H. Weedon	2 January 1950		Cinema
142 Saint Helier	T. P. Bennett & Son	2 June 1952	15 January 2009	Church
143 Westbourne Grove	Leonard Allen	29 August 1955	9 June 1986	1986
144 Highgate	T. P. Bennett & Son	19 December 1955	6 January 1973	1974
145 Sheffield	Robert Bullivant, H. Weedon	15 July 1956	5 June 1971	Bingo
1960s - under The Rank Organisation ownership - not part of this photo series				
146 Harlow	Robert Bullivant	1 August 1960	1 August 2005	Vacant
147 Hemil Hempstead	Harry Weedon Partnership	29 August 1960	1974	Pub
148 Leeds	Gillinson Barnet	17 August 1964	1 October 1977	Vacant
149 Nottingham	Harry Weedon Partnership	12 July 1965	26 January 2001	2012
150 Elephant & Castle	Ernö Goldfinger	22 December 1966	8 July 1988	1988
151 Marble Arch	Clifford Aish	2 February 1967	8 May 2016	2016
152 Swansea	Cassidy, Farrington & Dennys	17 May 1967	14 December 1997	2018
153 St Martins Lane	Richard Seifert	12 October 1967	7 June 1997	Gym
154 Stockton-on-Tees	Anthony Sharp (interior)	25 April 1968	24 October 1981	Vacant

REFERENCES

In addition to the specific quote references below, the importance of the two-volume set: Odeon Cinemas 1 & 2 by Allen Eyles in researching this project cannot be understated. Without the in-depth information presented in these works, producing Odeon Relics would have been a far more arduous task. If you are interested in studying the Odeon story in further detail, there is no better place to start.
ISBN: 978-0-851708-13-3 & 1-84457-048-7

A special mention should also go to the website www.cinematreasures.com. This online encyclopaedia of cinemas across the globe is an invaluable information source, and entries on Odeon cinemas (especially by Ken Roe) have again been extremely useful in tracing the history of each building through the decades.

A fitting large scale appraisal of John Maltby's life and work isn't presently available, but RIBA have published an excellent pocket book by Robert Elwall that is essential reading for those wishing to learn more about his photography.
ISBN 1-85946-082-8

Introduction (6-17):

1) cinemauk.org.uk data
2) Cinemas of the Black Country - Ned Williams
3) Gropuis - Lupfer & Sigel p18
4) Architectural Review - September 1926
5) Focus on Film, 1975
6) Form Follows Fun: Modernism and Modernity in British Pleasure Architecture p100
7) Eagle Star's Chairman, Sir Edward Mountain was also director of Odeon
8) The Property Masters: A History of the British Commercial Property Sector p89
9) For the exterior, Deutsch employed Nottingham-based Thomas Cecil Howitt
10) Odeon Leicester Square opening programme 02/11/37
11) Architectural Design & Construction, vol 7, 07/03/37
12) The amazing life of Birmingham-born cinema pioneer Oscar Deutsch - Business Live 30/05/13
13) Odeon Cavalcade Documentary - 1973
14) Elaine Harwood as interviewed by Jason Sayer
15) Casino Guardian 06/03/18

Odeon Relics (22-136):

1) Everyman: the chain pushing to bring home cinema to the high street – Guardian 05/08/16
2) HE List entry 1311970
3) Odeon Cinemas 1 – Allen Eyles p57
4) Odeon Cinemas 2 – Allen Eyles p160
5) Odeon Cavalcade Documentary - 1973
6) HE list entry 1271848
7) Homes, bars & restaurants planned for Mecca Bingo site: Kent Online 25/08/18
8) Selladoor press statement 09/03/19
9) modernistbritain.co.uk entry 01/05/14
10) Camden News Journal 15/03/18
11) HE List entry 1384944
12) diamondbandquettingsuite.com
13) British Listed Buildings – Apollo Cinema & Bingo Club
14) Odeon Cinemas 1 – Allen Eyles p96
15) Leicester Square Odeon to reopen after multi-million pound refit: Standard 08/11/18
16) Odeon Cinemas 1 – Allen Eyles p81
17) Britain's Oldest Unsolved Murder – Bristol Post 26/08/18
18) Odeon Cinemas 1 – Allen Eyles p164
19) Odeon lined up for move to Kyle Centre: Daily Record 30/11/15
20) HE List entry 1356878
21) Mecca Bingo Hall Outrages Muslims: Independent 07/0 /98
22) cinematreasures comments board 19/08/07

THANKS…

Philip would like to thank:

My wife Natasha and daughters Dorothy & Beatrice for tolerating some pretty weird family holidays dictated more by cinema location than anything else!
Also a huge thanks to the following, many of whom were instrumental in helping me realise this project: Jason Sayer, Joanne Halliday, Will Scott, Joshua Abbott, Lukas Novotny, Morely von Sternberg, Tom Padshaw, Alan & Marion Marshall, Mike Dawson, Greg Holmes, Patrick Fry, Colin Wilkinson, Elaine Harwood, David Trevor-Jones, Jessica Jenkinson, Christopher Beanland, Hillary Pye, Jessie-Ann Lewis, Ian Hay, Eric Knowles, Hira Ram, William Ratti, Paul Bains, Nancy Isherwood, Lionel Martin, Thomas Collison, Martin Carter, Oliver Bennett, Ian Mansfield, all the ADSocUK founders .. and everyone out there in social media-land for your support and encouragement!

Jason would like to thank:

Elaine Harwood, Historic England, The Twentieth Century Society, Dr Phil Wickham, The Bill Douglas Cinema Museum, University of Exeter, Anthony Cartwright, Author Nathan Abrams, Will Wiles, Bangor University.

ORGANISATIONS OF NOTE…

If you are passionate about historic cinemas, Twentieth Century architecture, or inter-war design, you might wish to consider joining one of the following organisations.

Cinema Theatre Association - "Dedicated to cinema history - not the films, but the buildings they were and are shown in". www.cinema-theatre.org.uk

Twentieth Century Society. From the International Style and Art Deco through to post-war gems like the Royal Festival Hall and designs such as the red telephone box, we aim to save and commemorate the best of the century. www.c20society.org.uk

Art Deco Society UK - a not-for-profit organisation bringing together lovers of Art Deco design from across the British Isles. www.artdecosociety.uk

SUPPORTERS LIST

The first publication of this book was partially financed by crowdfunding through the Kickstarter website. A special mention goes out to the lovely people listed below for contributing extra to have their names included within these pages.

Adam Tinworth • Adam Watson Brown • Alan Bennett • Alex Lee • Alex Woolfson • Andrew Jones
Andrew Wilson • Andy Dennison • Anthony Adams • Ben Farress-Noble • Ben Hodgson • Ben Packman
Brian Howell and Tim Adey • Bruce Steer • Cakes Baker • Chip, Karen and Ian Cox • Clare Dowse
Clive Stonebridge • Craig Travis • Damon Murray • Daniel Kardani-Zadeh • Darren Nuttall
David Bertram • David Bonney • David Lars Chamberlain • David Gregory • David Lawson
David Thistlethwaite • David Wilson • Diana Walkden • Dr Sarah Halton • Dr. Thomas Hurdsfield
Elain Harwood • Elizabeth Valenza • Ellen Cheshire • Emily Holworthy • Essy Gareth Negus
Gareth Phua • Gary Painter • Genista Davidson • Geoffrey Goddard • Gert-Jan Lobbes Greg Ivings
Greg Swan • Hadrien Esteve • Harry Clow • Hazel Nicholson • Hugh Gibbs • Iain Sturch
Ian Pleace • Isaiah Whisner • James Christopher Hill • James Fletcher • James Gratrix • James Whittell
Jennie Harrison • Jeremy Spencer • John Dixon • John Jones • John Maynard • John Skinner
Jon Guntrip • Jonathan Crown • Jonathan Rishton • Jonathan Walket • Jorren Schauwaert • Jules Curran
Julian & Giles Benton • Keith James • Keith Sherratt • Kevin Trickett MBE • Kristian Häring
Kristoffer Röine Larsson • L Rushing • Lauren Livesey • Lee Oatway • Leigh Stanford • Leshia Doucet
Lionel Martin • Lisa Bardsley • Lucy Jane Santos • Lukas Novotny • Lynn Slinger • made with volume
Marcel Westhoff • Margaret Hallah • Mark Dendy • Mark Fowkes • Mark Teece • Mark White
Mark Whyte • Martin John Carter • Martin Mckay • Martyn Grogan • Mathew Giles • Matthew Steele
Michael Gibson • Michael Jones • Michael Paley • Michael Payne • Michael Prince
Mike McCall • Mike Yates • Milan Poznanović • Mr Richard Thomas Rainbow • Nardia Miller
Natasha Chisdes • Neil Davies • Nicholas Aleksander • Nick Simmons • Oliver Herington • Olivier Jaeggi
Paul & Rhian Andrews • Paul Brackley • Paul Britcher • Paul Clements • Paul Dielemans
Paul Hill-Gibbins • Paul Smith • Paul Stewart • Paul Sutcliffe • Peter Hollick • Peter Humphries
Peter J. Knight • Phil Olsen • Philip Brown • Philip Storry • Pierre VINCENT • PJ McLavety • Post Utility
Preston Nyman • Qu Wenhao • Richard Ashman • Richard Coltman • Richard Gooding • Richard Himan
Richard Matthews • Richard Norman • Richard Salkeld • Rob Morton • Robert Cowan
Robert Kennedy • Robert Vaughan • Robin Kearney • Robin Rae • Roger Patenall • Rosalind Ryman
Roy Bent • Sam Manning • Samantha Brown • Sarah Wittekind • Shauna Barr
Sid Penance • Spencer Richards • Stéphane Deschamps • Steven Collins • Stephen Morris
Stephen Press • Steve Sykes • Steven Moschidis • Stuart Henderson • Suzi Lyon • Tamsin Hart-Jones
Thomas Padfield • Tim Abram • Tim Adams • Tony Binder • Toshiyuki Machida • Trevor Ingman
Wibbie • Wilco • Yẹmí Àlàdérun • Yvonne Budden • Yvonne Jewkes • @23an